THE HOUR OF SEHAR

A Memoir of Brokenness, Becoming, and the Love That Rewrote My Story

MELINDA S. JACKSON

This work is registered with the United States Copyright Office.
Registration number: TXu 2-511-426
Effective date of registration: June 30, 2025

Paperback ISBN: 979-8-9932088-0-0
Hardcover ISBN: 979-8-9932088-1-7
eBook ISBN: 979-8-9932088-2-4

Published by Sehar Press
Temple, Texas
United States of America

Cover design by Nick Castle
Interior formatting by Jonathan Lewis

First edition, 2026

Dedication

To the little girl I used to be,

I see you now.

You were never too much. Never a problem to fix. You were loud because you were silenced at home. You made people laugh because you were aching to be noticed. You filled rooms with energy because you were searching for a place to belong. You weren't a troublemaker; you were simply misunderstood. You belong. You are safe. You are seen.

And I understand you now.

To the young woman who mishandled people's hearts and built walls to protect herself, I forgive you. I grieve with you and for you. You were searching for something in the world that only God could give. The Lord lovingly and patiently waits for you, and He pursues your heart daily because you are worth it.

To the young mother who did the very best she could in survival mode. Your children remember the soft moments: they remember the compassion, the kindness, the tenderness, and the humor. They remember a mother who loves and protects them fiercely. It's evident in the young men they are becoming: their compassionate hearts and open minds, their love for Jesus and His people. The perfect mother doesn't exist, but you're doing great. Give yourself grace.

And now, to the woman standing in the light:
Put down the shame that was never yours to carry.
Step out from behind the walls you built to survive.
You are a daughter of the Most High God:
forgiven, restored, redeemed.
Walk boldly into the hour of your Sehar.
Your new beginning starts here.

Contents

"Even the darkness is not dark to You; the night shines like the day, for darkness is as light to You. For You formed my inward parts; You wove me together in my mother's womb. I praise You, for I am fearfully and wonderfully made … Your eyes saw my unformed body; all my days were written in Your book before one of them came to be."

— PSALM 139:12-16

Echoes in My Name

MY MIDDLE NAME, Seda, means *Echo* in Turkish; it was created from the first initials of the names of my mother and the man I believed was my father: **Se**val and **Da**vid. For most of my life, that name felt like a symbol of who I was, an echo of other people's choices, secrets, and silences.

David raised me. He fought for me. He promised to love me as his own. And for a long time, I believed that promise meant something simple: that I belonged to him. That I came from him. That my story began with his name.

But truth, like an echo, has a way of finding its way back.

At twenty-five, I learned that my biological father was someone else, a man named Hardy. I spoke to him only twice, both times he denied me completely, not just as his daughter but as a possibility for connecting. His rejection wasn't loud or dramatic. It was quiet. Clean. Final. And it left a familiar ache in its wake.

There were pieces of the story I couldn't reconcile: my mother's flawed honesty, the family's denials, the way everyone seemed committed to forgetting the version that included me. The more I reached for clarity, the more the truth slipped into shadows. Eventually, I stopped reaching for it.

But identity can sometimes unravel, even when we're determined to hold it together.

My childhood became a series of contradictions: belonging and unbelonging, affection and resentment, truth and secrecy. Summers spent with David were both beautiful and brittle. I wanted to believe I was wanted. Sometimes I was, sometimes I wasn't. I learned to move carefully in the spaces between.

There were years I felt like I was living in a name that didn't fit me, a life pieced together from other people's decisions. A life inherited rather than chosen.

But echoes can't last forever. At some point, they fade.

And in the quiet that follows, a new sound begins to rise.

This memoir is the story of that rise, the journey from echo to voice, from borrowed identity to inherited purpose, from the darkness of what I didn't know to the light of what I finally claimed.

It's the story of where I came from,

and the story of who I became.

CHAPTER 1

Dreams Come True in California?

I N THE LATE seventies, Army Specialist David Jackson was stationed in Istanbul, Turkey, far from his hometown of Coeur d'Alene, Idaho. The culture, the language, the smells of unfamiliar spices in the air all made the distance feel greater. He and his friend Bob tried to combat homesickness however they could, and for David, that meant spinning records as a DJ at the downtown Officers' Club. It was there, surrounded by the glow of neon lights and the hum of a foreign city, that he saw her.

Two women entered the club and scanned the room before finding seats at the bar. One of them, short, olive-skinned, eyes lined with kohl, caught David's attention. "Your mother," he used to say, with a distant look in his eyes, "was the most beautiful woman I had ever seen. I would've done anything to make her smile." That line didn't go over well with my stepmother, especially when he said it in front of her, but David never forgot.

In my teenage years, I remember catching him watching me sometimes, his expression unreadable. "You know, kid," he'd murmur, "you're really starting to look like your mother." There was something both tender and heavy in those moments, like he was talking to her through me. And from the next room, as if on cue, my stepmother would grumble, "And act like her too…" as if that were some kind of insult. She claimed I had a "smart mouth," a trait I apparently inherited from my mother, but I think what truly bothered her was that I reminded David of someone he never stopped loving.

David wasn't a man of conventionally charming looks. He was short, balding, and wore thick Army-issued glasses known among soldiers as BCGs, "birth control glasses." But he was persistent, and when he learned through the bartender that my mother loved Kenny Rogers, he made his move. That night, he played nothing but Kenny Rogers: "Lucille," "The Gambler," "Sweet Music Man," and "Love Lifted Me," each song a stepping-stone toward her smile. And he earned it, along with a date the following week.

Turkey, while predominantly Muslim, had pockets of Western influence at the time. Turkish families were fiercely protective of their daughters, especially when it came to American GIs stationed nearby. David eventually met my grandparents, bringing offerings of fruit and American whiskey from the local American base's Class Six. He formally asked for permission to date their daughter, and, in time, for their blessing to marry her. Everyone loved David: his warmth, his attentiveness, his American charm. My mother fell in love with the idea of him and America.

Within months, my mother was dressed in an elaborate white lace gown, and David wore a cream and white silk suit, the first and, without a doubt, the last suit he ever wore outside of his Army dress greens, for their three-day wedding celebration. This was typical of Turkish culture, where the joy of marriage is shared with the entire town. While in Turkey, under the watchful eye of my mother's family, David treated Seval like a princess, always doting on her, showering her with gifts, love letters, and tender words of endearment. He was every bit the gentleman she had imagined spending the rest of her life with. Until he wasn't.

Two years later, pregnant with my sister Pamela, she boarded a military cargo plane and left her country behind for Copperas Cove, Texas. The change did not come gradually but happened in transit. Once the plane lifted from Turkish soil and the protection of family, culture, and witnesses fell away, so did the man she thought she had married. Somewhere over the Atlantic, she realized she had made a terrible mistake, as David had changed. The tenderness vanished, replaced by impatience, criticism, and control. He grew increasingly controlling, refusing to let her get a driver's license. He restricted her phone calls, even to family back in Turkey, claiming she spent too much time on the phone and not enough time cooking and cleaning. He also rarely allowed her to leave the house, and his temper became something she feared.

I experienced the contrast myself, the two faces of the same man. One day he was kind and generous, the man who would give a stranger the shirt off his back. The next, he was a red-faced storm of rage. "It's my way or the highway," he'd yell. And he meant it.

While I don't condone my mother's choices, born from a deep desire for freedom and longing, I've come to understand them. She was young, thousands of miles from everything familiar, trapped in a version of life that felt more like captivity than love.

She found comfort in two fellow Turkish Army wives, Sadiye and Mena, whose husbands were also stationed at Fort Hood. They became her lifeline to freedom and laughter. The three of them, vibrant, bold, and alluring, brought glamour to the dullness of military life. When they walked into a room, people noticed. They carried a beauty rarely seen outside of another world, the kind only ever printed on magazine covers or flashing across television screens. The mysteries of the Mediterranean were buried deep in their dark, almond-shaped eyes, and it was like a magnet, particularly for American men, even though they were married.

And that's when she met Hardy: older, more refined, an officer, and he treated her like a lady. He called her his "little Turkish flower," brought her gifts, and while David was busy working long hours, Seval would sneak away to spend time with Hardy. He picked her up in his flashy orange Porsche 911. He opened doors for her, treated her gently, and made her feel wanted. Their affair was brief but intoxicating, as she loved driving through the entrance gate at Fort Hood with him. The soldiers on duty would welcome him with respect and dignity, saluting him sharply. She would joke, "I really like it when they do that," to which Hardy would smile and ask when they did what. She explained that she loved when the officers saluted him, when they acknowledged his importance, and by extension, made her feel important too. He would laugh and say, "Alright, my Turkish flower, let's go through again!" And he would make a quick U-turn, leave the base, and re-enter so she could experience it one more time. She felt lighthearted around him, like a schoolgirl.

But beneath the surface, something deeper was happening: my mother's hunger for respect and importance collided with Hardy's playful but ultimately shallow affection, giving her the brief illusion of the dignity she craved so badly. It is a dangerous thing, longing for rescue from someone who was never meant to be your savior.

The affair continued for months, stolen hours of affection that felt like safety in a world where she felt she had none. Then, one day, she told Hardy she was pregnant. With me. She braced herself for rejection, for blame, for abandonment, but instead, he promised her a new life. A fresh start. He said he would take care of her and the baby, set her up with an apartment in California, help her start over. No more cold silences. No more slammed doors. No more living under David's control. And she believed him, not because she was naive but because she was desperate. Desperate for escape. Desperate to be chosen. Desperate to believe that Hardy loved her enough to rescue her.

In a small military town in Texas, under the weight of everything she couldn't say, my mother left. She left her baby girl, Pamela, with her friend Mena while David was at work and ran toward a future she so desperately wanted to be real. But it wasn't just her life that had been torn open. My sister, barely a year old, had been left behind. Left to wonder, even if she didn't have the words for it yet, why the one person who was supposed to stay had disappeared.

Seval chose herself. When you're drowning, you don't stop to weigh the cost. You just swim; you just run; you save the life you think you can still save. Maybe she thought she could outrun the consequences. Maybe she believed that if she could just reach freedom, she could fix what was broken later. But broken things have a way of bleeding into everything they touch, and the choice she made in that moment would scar us all for decades to come.

Desperation clouds reason. Fear drowns out love. Shame builds walls where there should have been bridges. Seval wasn't chasing hope; she was fleeing captivity. But David was still a soldier. And soldiers don't surrender easily.

When David arrived home after work that evening and realized Seval was gone, the mask came off. He didn't plead. He didn't reason. He threatened; if she didn't come back, he said, she would never see her daughter Pamela again. The weight of that threat crushed whatever hope she had carried out the door.

After only a few days in California, days that must have felt like living between two broken worlds, she came back to Texas. Defeated. Angry. Filled with regret. The resentment toward David took root quickly. It festered in her, turning everything bitter, and what had started as an escape now morphed into a silent war she couldn't win.

Just days after returning to Texas, David came home to find Mena at the house with Pamela. But my mother was gone, again. She had taken Mena's car and driven to an abortion clinic, trying to erase the evidence of her betrayal. Trying to make it all go away. But Mena, knowing the spiritual and emotional cost this would have on my mother, and on her family in Turkey, told David the truth about the affair and pregnancy.

He drove to the clinic with the urgency of a man on a mission. And what happened next, I have played over in my mind so many times. It feels like my own memory, even though I wasn't there. He walked into that waiting room and saw her crying, terrified, alone. And instead of unleashing the anger he was known for, he sat beside her. He took her hand, lifted her chin, and said, "Let's go, we'll figure this out. I promise I'll love and raise this baby like my own." Somehow, grace broke through rage. And 8 months later, in July 1982, I was born.

There's only one baby photo of David and me. He's holding me, grinning from ear to ear, and I'm in a yellow polka dot dress, hands on his chest, eyes wide and curious. Even now, tears blur my vision when I think of that picture. As a little girl, I would pull out the photo album, find that image, close my eyes, and imagine a father who loved me like that all the time. A father who smiled often. A father who made me feel like I belonged.

As a gesture of their commitment to raise me together, they gave me a name that carried both of them: "Se" from Seval and "Da" from David, Seda. In Turkish and Arabic, Seda means "echo." At the time, no one could have known how prophetic that name would be, but I grew up hearing that echo. Carrying it. Living it. Repeating the pain that preceded me, even when I didn't understand its origin. I didn't just inherit their features; I inherited their unfinished story. I didn't know it then, but I was born carrying an echo. And I would hear it for years to come.

CHAPTER 2

God Was Watching

THE RESENTMENT THEY carried between each other was too much to hold. Less than a year after I was born, David and my mother divorced. Whatever fragile thread had held their union together had finally snapped, and the promise to raise me together unraveled just as quickly as it had been made.

During her pregnancy with me, my mother's father, my grandfather Hakki, passed away in Turkey. She was too far along to travel, and the grief of being unable to attend his funeral only deepened the isolation she already felt in America. So, when the divorce was finalized, and I was almost a year old, she returned to Turkey, with my sister and I, to mourn her father, to reconnect with her roots, and to breathe in the familiarity of home. What began as a temporary visit, became something more permanent.

Back in her homeland, surrounded by family and the comfort of her native language and culture, I imagine she felt a momentary sense of relief. For the first time in years, she wasn't watched, monitored, or silenced. She could grieve openly, move freely, and begin to stitch herself back together in the places where marriage and betrayal had torn her apart.

During those years in Turkey, my sister and I were folded into a kind of tenderness that existed only within the walls of my mother's childhood home. My aunts, Meral and Nehal, understood the weight of what my mother would face: shame, whispers, judgment, and the burden of returning with two daughters and a fractured marriage. They tried, in their own ways, to shield us from the treatment. I don't remember much from that time, just fragments offered back to me through stories told later. My aunt Nehal, who had two sons and longed for a daughter, once asked if she could keep me and raise me as her own. However, my mother refused with a fierceness that surprised even them. Still, they doted on us. Pamela, with her bright blonde hair, sun-kissed freckles, and wide American smile, was called the "little American baby." And I, with features mirroring my mother's, was known as the Turkish baby. For a brief season, we were cherished, wrapped in affection, belonging completely to a family trying to steady itself under the weight of what came next.

While we were in Turkey, David received a change of duty station and relocated to Fort Lewis, Washington. The peace my mother had found was short-lived. David harassed her relentlessly, threatening to have her arrested if she didn't return his children.

I wish I could believe it was love that made him so desperate to have us back, but experience tells a different story. David had an older son from his first marriage and had little, if any, relationship with him beyond a monthly child support check. I wish I could believe it was about us, but I know better. His anger, his threats, they weren't acts of fatherly love. They were about power. About control. About not letting her go.

After a few years in Turkey, and under mounting threats and legal pressure from David, my mother had no choice but to return to the U.S. with us. We relocated to Auburn, Washington. As a single mother now myself, I see her circumstances through a different lens. She spoke very little English. She had no friends, no family nearby, no job, no higher education. And yet, she was expected to raise two daughters in a country that had never made room for her.

I don't remember much of the first five years of my life, but I know we were very poor. We lived in a government-subsidized townhouse complex, with a food bank just across the street. My mother worked two jobs, and when we weren't in school, my sister and I were mostly alone.

She took vacations with the men she dated, one I remember took her to Hawaii for over a week, and when she returned, she brought gifts: shirts with beads, coconut shells, and flowered lays that almost made up for the fact that she left us with no food and no way to contact her; this was long before cellphones or check-ins. Somehow, by the grace of God and the kindness of strangers, we stayed alive.

What I didn't understand then was how much my sister had been robbed of her childhood. She wasn't just fending for herself; she was taking care of me. Pamela became my anchor far earlier than any child should, and that seemed to be the theme of our early adolescence: experiencing life, hardship, and trauma long before we were ready.

My mother did try, in her own way, to plan for our care when she wasn't going to be around for long periods. But any parent will tell you, even the best-laid plans can fall apart. One of those plans came in the form of our next-door neighbor, Lindi.

Lindi worked the counter at the nearby 7-Eleven, and she was hard to miss: tall and broad with a thick gray mullet, always smelling of cigarettes and sipping on a Big Gulp of Dr. Pepper. She was also a single mother to a teenage daughter who shared her name. We called them Big Lindi and Little Lindi. Big Lindi was intimidating, strict, and blunt. But Little Lindi? She was everything I thought was cool and glamorous. At 16, she looked like she had stepped straight out of a late-80s Madonna music video.

And for anyone who doesn't know what that era of Madonna looked like, let me paint the picture: puffy skirts layered over neon leggings, denim jackets, crimped hair and sky-high bangs, electric blue and hot pink eyeshadow, lace gloves, and an army of scrunchies. She hadn't yet stepped into the "Vogue" era. She was all attitude and eyeliner, and I idolized her.

They both babysat Pamela and me after school until our mother came home from work. If Big Lindi was off work, we mostly stayed in our house, and she would check in periodically. But if she was at the store, I'd go hang out at their place with Little Lindi and her friends. I was seven years old and already learning how to roll tin foil pipes around pencils so I could smoke with the older kids.

One day, I even stole a little weed from their stash and brought it home, feeling proud of myself. I showed my sister how to make a makeshift bong out of a used 2-liter soda bottle. She took one hit, nearly threw up, and swore she would tell our mother. Looking back, it's heartbreaking. I wasn't a rebellious kid; I was a lonely, little girl trying to find identity and connection wherever I could. And Little Lindi made me feel like I mattered. I felt cool around her. I felt seen.

I had spent the weeks coloring at their kitchen table, watching Little Lindi talking and smoking with her guy friends and trying to copy her. I wanted to be like her: bold, pretty, impossible to ignore. I wore my new black and white dress that day at their house. I felt proud, like maybe I was getting closer to being more like her. I hoped she would notice; I hoped someone would. With that dress, I believed I would get her attention, anyone's attention. And I did, but not the kind of attention any little girl should experience.

Lindi asked me if I wanted to smoke with them, and I was excited to be included. Later that day, I had gotten so high, I could barely move. I was lying on their living room couch, heavy-limbed and foggy. That same black and white dress felt different now. What had made me feel special just hours earlier no longer offered any protection. Suddenly, I started to feel the weight of a body pressing into mine.

One of Little Lindi's guy friends was on top of me. He was lifting my dress, touching me, and kissing me. I was barely conscious, my mind detached from what was happening. I could hear Little Lindi's voice somewhere in the background, laughing, saying something like, "Melinda has a boyfriend." This couldn't be bad, right? But everything in me screamed that it was. I felt sick. I felt paralyzed. I felt terrified. And yet, I also felt this unbearable fear that if I protested, if I pushed him away, I wouldn't be wanted around anymore. That Lindi wouldn't want me around. So, I stayed silent as long as I could until he began to undress me. That's when my body woke up, and I screamed.

I screamed for him to stop, and I ran out of the apartment. I bolted into our house and crawled under my bed, my hiding place when the world felt too scary to face. Pamela was at a friend's house, so I stayed there, shaking and alone, until my mother returned from work later that evening. I told her what happened. Or, at least, I tried to. I'm still not sure if she understood me. She didn't hug me. She didn't ask questions. She didn't seem upset with Lindi or her friends; she seemed upset with me. I was confused, as I did nothing wrong. I remember her saying, almost with exasperation, "Well, who's going to babysit you two now?"

That night, she told us to come straight home after school and lock the door behind us. If someone knocked, we weren't to answer and pretend no one was home. It wasn't comfort. It wasn't safety. It was management; that was the day I learned that telling the truth could be dangerous. That sometimes it was easier to hide the real story and tell people what they wanted to hear.

It was also the day I learned something else, something that would haunt me for years: that I could use my body to get attention. Not attention that felt good or affirming, but attention that, in its own twisted way, filled the void of being unseen. A dark seed was planted that day in me, one of confusion, shame, and misplaced worth. It was an echo of the pain and loneliness my mother had buried in herself. And now, it had found its way into me.

That year, David returned to Fort Hood, Texas. By then, my mother had a fragile but growing support system and refused to move back to Texas. Instead, she agreed to send my sister and me to visit David each summer for a month, always on his dime. I remember that summer of 1990 especially well. David had been deployed in support of Operation Desert Storm, and that year, we didn't go to see him in Texas.

My mother was furious at this news. She had her own vacation plans, and our canceled trip disrupted them. She would say to her friends, "Damn Saddam Hussein!" Not because of the terrible dictator he was, but because he caused a war in Kuwait, and that interrupted her regularly scheduled summer programming. I remember feeling confused, scared, and sad. I looked forward to Texas, not because it was perfect but because I felt seen there. David always gave me a birthday party, since my birthday happened during that time. My sister's birthday was in January, but she always received gifts on mine, something I hated at the time but understand now.

One day back at home, my eighth birthday began like any other day. My mother was gone, and we didn't know where: at work, across the ocean, with a friend, or asleep beside someone new. There was no "Happy Birthday," no cake, no presents. Not even breakfast.

My sister wanted to ride bikes to a friend's house; I didn't. Instead, I walked across the street to the food bank. A kind, old man worked there, someone who had always treated me gently. People were lined up out front, but he often let me in through the back. I told him it was my birthday and asked if he had anything I could use to make a cake. He gave me groceries but no cake mix. At eight, I didn't know another way to bake one.

He looked at me with sorrow and tenderness, pulled me into a long hug, and whispered, "Happy birthday." He didn't ask about my mother or our plans. He didn't need to. I think he already knew.

Later that afternoon, my sister returned and called out for me to help her with a box left at the front door. Inside were two gift-wrapped packages, a birthday cake with candles, two stuffed Care Bears, and two sets of coloring books and crayons.

The kind man from the food bank had gone to the store and created a birthday party in a box. It wasn't the kind of celebration I'd had in Texas, but it was something sacred, an act of quiet love from someone who owed us nothing.

My sister found a lighter in the kitchen, lit the candles, and softly told me to make a wish. My wish didn't come true, but Pamela and I ate cake until we were sick, stayed up late coloring, and played with our new Care Bears. How perfectly poetic that gift, a reminder that in a world where children often feel alone and overlooked, someone, somewhere still cares.

That day, through someone kind, someone safe, someone who showed up for children with nothing, I experienced the heart and hands of Jesus without knowing Him, but He knew me.

For I was hungry and you gave Me something to eat, I was thirsty and you gave Me something to drink, I was a stranger and you invited Me in, I needed clothes and you clothed Me, I was sick and you looked after Me, I was in prison and you came to visit Me... Truly I tell you, whatever you did for one of the least of these brothers and sisters of Mine, you did for Me.

—MATTHEW 25:35, 40 (NKJV)

Selah

S ELAH APPEARS OVER SEVENTY times in the book of Psalms. While its exact meaning isn't known, many scholars agree it was a musical or poetic pause, a call to stop, reflect, and let the weight of what was just spoken settle in the soul. If you've made it this far, I want to take a moment to say, "Breathe." These chapters were difficult to write, so I imagine it may have been just as hard to read as well.

Revisiting childhood trauma, especially abuse, abandonment, and the pain of feeling unseen, isn't just storytelling; it's soul work. There were moments I had to stop mid-sentence and grieve all over again. And in one of those moments, God showed up most unexpectedly.

My cat Raya, whose name means "friend," is usually indifferent and aloof. She doesn't like being held or cuddled. But after I wrote a particularly painful scene, she climbed into my lap and curled up in my arms. It was as if she knew. As if the comfort I didn't know I needed found me through something soft, quiet, and present.

That morning, my verse of the day was Philippians 2:13 (NIV): "For it is God who works in you to will and to act to fulfill His good purpose." That wasn't a coincidence but a whisper from Heaven, a reminder that I am not alone in this work, and neither are you.

So, dear reader, if you are carrying pain like mine, or perhaps pain you've never shared aloud, I want to gently encourage you: Your story matters. Your healing matters. And you do not have to carry it alone. Talk to someone. A faith-based counselor, a trusted friend, a pastor, someone who can sit with your story and honor it. And talk to God. Invite Him into those tender places. He's already there, waiting to walk you through it.

Maybe there's a book in you. Maybe your story will be the very thing that unlocks freedom for someone else the way I pray this one will. But even if it's just between you and God for now, that's more than enough.

Selah. Take a moment. Let it settle.
You are not forgotten.
You are not alone.
You are deeply loved.

CHAPTER 3

Louder Than Silence

THERE ARE SADLY many stories of neglect and abuse I could share from my life, but I don't want this chapter, or this memoir, to be about suffering for suffering's sake. The truth is pain was only ever part of my story. There were glimmers of compassion, moments of genuine concern that surfaced even in the most unexpected places. One of those moments came during the summer of 1991.

David retired from the military and began planting roots in Belton, Texas, starting an electrical business that quickly began to thrive. Owning his own company had always been a dream of his, and by all accounts, he seemed happy. He eventually remarried, this time to a German woman named Norma, who had a teenage son of her own named Christopher. That summer, my mother traveled to Turkey following the death of her mother, my grandmother, Emina. While she was overseas, mourning and settling family matters with her sisters, we went to Texas to spend the summer with David.

At some point during our stay, David overheard Pamela and me talking, just being kids, swapping life stories back home. We didn't realize we were saying anything shocking. But to David, it was horrifying. The stories we told, the nights we were left alone, the days we had no food, the times we didn't know where our mother was, they made him visibly ill. For the first time, I saw something in his eyes that looked like genuine heartbreak. He sat us down and asked, "Do you want to stay here? Do you want to live in Texas with me?"

I remember feeling confused. Torn. There was something comforting about being asked; something in me wanted to believe this meant he cared. What I didn't know at the time was that my mother had already sent him a letter from Turkey, asking if he would keep my sister and me that year so she could remain in Turkey with her family a while longer. He hadn't told us yet, but the plan was already in motion. We were enrolled in school that fall.

I really didn't know how to feel about not going back home to Seattle. I was disoriented, confused by everything: new school, new house, new rules. And I missed my mother a lot. I was used to her being gone a lot, but at some point, she always came home. But this was different; I had no idea when I would see her again; that created an ache that lasted far beyond my confusion.

My stepmother, Norma, was cold and unwelcoming, and the culture shock was real. Up until that point, we knew nothing about God. We had never heard of Jesus. We had never eaten pork. Now, suddenly, bacon and pork chops were staples in the home, and every Sunday and Wednesday, we were required to go to a little Pentecostal church in town. It was all so strange, but even more difficult than the cultural shift was the change in David. He was no longer the softhearted, doting father I remembered from the summers. He was angry, short-tempered, and demanding. Structure was forced on us like we were new recruits in basic training; after years with no rules at all, the sudden rigidity felt like punishment.

Eventually, I came to love going to church, but not because I had any real understanding of Jesus or spiritual truth. I loved it because it gave me a break. A break from the yelling. A break from the slapping. A break from the names I was called. David and Norma became completely different people at church: warm, kind, and respectable. They smiled. They laughed. They played the part well. And at church, we were allowed to socialize a little. To have friends. To breathe, sometimes. However, even that was taken away from me at times, too.

That season was difficult for both Pamela and me, but if you asked her today, she'd tell you I had it worse. She was never afraid to admit how cruelly I was treated compared to her, but she also wasn't afraid to tell me that I didn't help matters. I always talked back; I got in trouble; I made things worse.

I didn't understand myself back then. The awareness we have today around trauma and how it affects young children didn't exist in the early nineties, certainly not in homes like ours. But looking back, I'm almost certain I was neurodivergent. Maybe ADD. Maybe ADHD. I was impulsive, forgetful, and socially awkward. I was also funny, charismatic, and passionate about anything that sparked my interest. I was just a kid trying to be a kid.

To David and Norma, though, I wasn't a child to understand. I was a problem to manage. A troublemaker. The black sheep. The one who couldn't behave, who talked too much, who never seemed to fit the mold they wanted. "Children are to be seen, not heard," Norma would often say.

But I wasn't loud because I wanted attention. I was loud because I was hurting. I was a confused, little girl desperate to be seen, desperate to be understood, desperate for someone to notice that something wasn't right.

And no matter how hard I tried, I never felt like I got anything right.

So eventually, I did the only thing that seemed to protect me: I stopped trying to be understood and started trying to survive.

Meanwhile, what was supposed to be a one-year stay in Texas quietly stretched into several. There was never a call, never a letter letting us know when, or if, we'd return to Washington with our mother. After a certain point, I stopped asking; the disappointing response from David, of "She hasn't returned our calls or written a response to our letters" was just too much disappointment for any child to endure repeatedly.

As I grew older, especially into my teenage years, the dynamics in the house became more difficult. One of the hardest parts was the loss of autonomy, even over things I had worked hard for. I held down two jobs while in high school, during long summers and late nights, and yet, I wasn't allowed to have a checking account and manage the money I earned. I had to turn over my paychecks to Norma and ask for money as if it wasn't mine. Sometimes when I'd ask to buy something simple, something I had rightfully earned, I'd hear, "You don't need that," or "You don't have enough." But I knew I did.

So, I tried to keep track of the money, but much of it seemed to disappear. I began to suspect, and later, learned that some of it was quietly being passed along to my stepbrother. David and Norma often argued about her giving him money without telling David, and redirecting my earnings was her way around that conflict. It was a confusing and helpless position to be in, chipping away at my sense of trust and independence. Over time, resentment began to take root in places I wish it never had. And yet, I continued striving to earn Norma's acceptance.

Norma often baked for our church's potlucks and bake sales, and her German chocolate cake was especially prized. She would make several cakes at a time, moving swiftly around the kitchen. I would sit at the bar, asking if I could help mix or prep, but she never wanted my help. "Just stay out of my way," she would snap, barely glancing at me. So, I did my best to stay invisible.

One Saturday, David called her from a jobsite, yelling through the phone loud enough for me to hear from my room. He needed a part delivered immediately to the jobsite. Everything with David was urgent, and he demanded she drop everything to bring it to him. The cakes were already baking in the oven, and I was the only one left at home. Norma called out to me, "I need your help." I couldn't believe it. After years of feeling like a burden, I was finally being trusted with something important.

My heart raced with both fear and excitement. Norma quickly explained that the cakes were set on a timer, and when the timer went off, I was to simply take them out and place them on the cooling racks, nothing more. Easy enough. I reassured her that I understood, and she rushed out the door.

I sat by the oven, staring through the window, watching the cakes rise. I could smell the rich chocolate, see the cakes rising over the top of the pans. But then I panicked; it looked like they were done, even though the timer hadn't gone off yet. I worried they might burn. Afraid to mess up, afraid to disappoint her, I pulled the cakes out early. As I set them on the cooling racks, the centers collapsed, sinking into themselves like popped balloons. In a panic, I shoved them back into the oven, praying they would fix themselves, but it was too late. What had fallen could not rise again.

Norma returned about thirty minutes later. I was hiding in my room, heart pounding. I heard her slam her purse onto the counter, followed by the sharp clatter of pans. "Mel!" she screamed. "What the hell did you do?" I shuffled out, head hung low. I couldn't meet her eyes at first, but when I finally looked up, her face was flushed with rage. I stumbled through my explanation, trying to tell her what happened. Then she slapped my face. Hard. So hard it felt like my skin tore open. I don't know what hurt worse, my face or the moment she screamed in my face, "What are you, stupid or something? This is why I tell you to stay out of my way. You can't get anything right."

Tears streamed down my face as I backed away into my room. I heard her on the phone yelling at David, her voice rising like she was proud of what she'd done: "You know what your stupid daughter did..." I felt so small and wanted to disappear completely. It was just a cake. A mistake. Cakes can be replaced, but I was never just punished for mistakes. I was punished for existing wrong.

What I didn't understand then, I see so clearly now. Norma carried her own bitterness, her own unresolved pain. She had made hard choices in life, and instead of brushing the dust off her feet and moving forward, she stayed bitter. And David, volatile and controlling, only added fuel to the fire inside her. They were miserable peas in a pod, two deeply wounded people who only knew how to wound others. Even now, as an adult, I try to have a relationship with Norma. But the bitterness is still there: heavy, oppressive, unavoidable. My children even felt it from them. Something about being in that house always felt heavy. Dark.

Eventually, I had to set firm boundaries and went no contact, to protect me and my children's peace.

But not every memory from their house was filled with pain. My stepbrother, who had a bit of a defiant streak like I did, thought the way Norma treated me was unfair. Even he recognized it, and she was his mother. He was older and quiet about it all, but I think he saw more than he let on.

Every Christmas, we would get the Kay-Bee-Toys and K-Mart ads and cut out the pictures for our wish lists. What I wanted wasn't in those ads; it was in the new RadioShack catalog. I had seen it during the commercials between Saturday morning cartoons, a remote-controlled car called the Ricochet. Sleek and fast like a European sports car, but with off-road tires that made it perfect for the gravel roads and dirt patches on our property.

We had all worked hard decorating our lists, taping and gluing our cutouts onto sheets of notebook paper. Norma walked by the table and snatched mine off without a second glance. She started laughing. "You're not getting this. This is for boys. Are you a boy?" Pamela sat quietly, avoiding eye contact with me out of fear, as I searched her face for compassion and understanding. But my stepbrother quickly shot back, "Who cares? It's what she wants for Christmas!" Norma threw him a glare. He just looked at me with sadness. Then, without a word, she crumpled my list into a ball and tossed it into the trash. "She'll be lucky if she gets a box of coal this year," she muttered.

At that moment, I ran from the table to my room, tears already spilling down my cheeks. I passed David, who was sitting in his chair, completely disengaged, watching an old John Wayne movie. As I shut my door, I heard him yell, "What the hell is her problem?" "She's mad because she's not going to get what she wants," Norma called back. Then came the familiar phrase I had heard from David far too many times over the years: "If she wants to cry, I'll give her something to cry about!"

I wasn't allowed to be happy. I wasn't allowed to be sad. I wasn't allowed to make noise. I wasn't allowed to be seen. It was hard to even breathe in that house without being picked apart. Even though it was clear to anyone who spent time there how I was treated, no one ever spoke up for me. I never understood why people were too afraid to say something, to stand up for me. But that Christmas, my stepbrother did.

On Christmas morning, I didn't wake up with the usual excitement of discovering packages from my wish list, but I was grateful for anything I received. Truly. My stepbrother handed me a box and said, "This one has your name on it, but doesn't say who it's from. Must be from Santa." He gave me a wink and a smile.

Excitement lit up my face and pulsed through my whole body. I heard Norma ask, "What is that?" I was afraid to hope, but I dared to dream it might be the one thing I had asked for before my list was thrown away. I tore away the wrapping just enough to reveal the Ricochet car inside the box. My stepbrother had already removed the plastic ties and screws from the packaging. He had even installed the batteries in both the car and the remote. As soon as I opened the box, I raced outside to play with it, ignoring the rest of the unopened gifts under the tree.

At that moment, he was Santa! Christopher gave me something more than just a toy. He gave me joy. He gave me validation. He gave me the feeling that someone saw me and believed I mattered.

During this time in Texas, my mother was largely absent from my life. Communication was sporadic at best, as she never wrote, hardly ever sent packages, and rarely called. And when she did, it almost always triggered an argument between me and David or Norma. When my mother called, it was never to ask about my life. There was no real concern, no curiosity, only what felt like a desperate attempt to ease her guilt. She would say things like, "I want to come see you both so bad, but David won't let me. He says he'll throw me in jail if I even come to Texas!" Even if that were true, which could very well be, you don't tell your children that.

Parents are supposed to shield and protect their kids from that sort of nonsense. Every time she called, I would get off the phone feeling angry and confused. I'd lash out at Norma and David for taking us away from her, for keeping her from us. I carried the weight of her words, and that was far too much for any child. While she seemed to be off creating a new life for herself, we were left trying to make sense of our own, without her.

One Sunday after church, we had extended family from out of town visiting, and Norma was outside grilling while David was sitting in his chair half-asleep, half watching a prerecorded Nascar race on TV. The kids were all running around outside playing a violent redneck version of hide-and-go seek. We took our beloved tube socks, it was a nineties thing and filled a quarter of each one with rocks, sticks, leaves, more rolled-up tube socks, whatever we could get our hands on. Then we'd tie them shut so the stuffing wouldn't fall out and use them as weapons. There was no gentle, "Tag, you're it!" You got an unsuspecting smack from the "homie sock," what we called these socks. We were outside laughing and having a blast when the phone rang inside the house.

My mother called for the second time that afternoon. I happened to be walking into the house to use the bathroom and overheard Norma answering the phone. "They're not home, Seval. Quit calling!" she said and then hung up. I looked at her with pure disgust. "What are you doing? Don't tell my mother not to call again!" I yanked the cordless phone out of her hand, ran to my room, and locked the door behind me. I called my mother back, told her I was home, and asked if she was okay. It was the first time I had heard from her in months, and I was desperate to talk to her.

I asked how she was, and she told me she was in Turkey with her new boyfriend, then started talking about how they met. But less than a minute into the call, she said, "I'm sorry, we're sitting down for dinner. I'll call you later," and hung up. No "I miss you." No "I love you." No "Are you both okay?" Just her voice talking about a man, then a dial tone. I was so furious I threw the phone on the floor and ran out of my room, straight past Norma, and outside to the barn in our neighbor's property. That's where I'd go to feed the cows and donkey while trying to calm myself down. To ground myself.

After about an hour, I heard Norma calling for me, telling me it was time to eat. Everyone else had already eaten, but she had saved a plate for me. I sat down at the table, my face still red and swollen from crying. She brought me a Dr. Pepper and said, more softly than I had ever heard her speak, "I told her not to call because I knew it would make you upset. You and your sister were outside playing and so happy. I didn't want to ruin that." I was too angry to understand that was her way of showing kindness. I couldn't see it, not then. I had so much anger in my heart, and I didn't know what to do with it. So, I just sat there in silence and ate the plate of barbecue, with extra deviled eggs, because she knew I liked them.

That's what made Norma's abuse so difficult to make sense of. She could be so cruel, so cold, and then she'd do something like saving me extra deviled eggs or speaking softly for once, and it gave me hope. Hope that maybe I could be a daughter to her. Hope that maybe she could be a mother to me. And for a long time, I clung to that hope like a lifeline. It kept me striving for perfection, bending over backwards to earn her love. But it was never enough. No matter how well I behaved, how hard I worked, how much I tried, it was never enough.

I spent so many years trying to earn love from women who didn't know how to give it. Norma was there but didn't want me. Seval wanted me, or said she did, but wasn't there. And in between them, I kept contorting myself, hoping that if I just got it right, one of them might choose me fully, but neither of them ever did. Not really.

Years later, without warning, my mother showed up in Texas. I was working at Blockbuster Video when I looked up to find her standing at my register, a friend beside her. I later learned she had told this friend that David had taken us from her, and that this surprise visit was the only way she could see her daughters. It was one of the most surreal moments of my life. I hadn't seen my mother in almost a decade. Suddenly, there she was, standing in front of me while I rang up customers. I was caught completely off guard, unsure of what to say or how to feel. The first words that came out of my mouth were, "What are you doing here?" She tried to tell me a story about how David kept us away from her; probably the same imagined story she told the friend who was with her. I told her that this was not the time or place for this, and I needed to return to my responsibilities at work, as I didn't know what else to say to her. So she left.

It was deeply uncomfortable. I wasn't the little girl who used to wait by the window for her anymore. I had grown into someone she didn't know, someone shaped by years of absence, silence, and unanswered questions. I had learned to live without her; I didn't feel joy toward her. I felt confusion. I felt grief. I felt the weight of a relationship that never had the chance to grow. As hard as it was to admit, I didn't miss her, not in the way I once did. Too much had happened. Too much had been left unspoken. We were strangers to each other. And that, more than anything, was what broke my heart.

CHAPTER 4

Where The Roots Lie

MOST PEOPLE DO not lie because they are bad; they lie because they are scared. That fear can take all kinds of shapes: fear of getting into trouble, fear of making a parent angry, fear of not being accepted, fear of being seen as less than. Sometimes, kids lie to protect themselves; other times, they lie to fit in. They make things up to impress their friends, or they cover up a mistake they are too ashamed to admit. Underneath it all, there is usually a deep and very human desire to be safe and to be loved.

I've caught my sons in lies, and although I'm baffled at their audacity in attempting to lie to their human lie detector mom, I always try to give them the benefit of the doubt or a small window of amnesty. I do not rush to judgment. I look for the fear. I look for the story underneath. Because behind most lies, there is a child who is still learning how to manage a world that feels too big, too fast, and sometimes too unforgiving. And more than punishment, what that child often needs is patience, guidance, and the kind of love that sees through the behavior and into the heart.

I certainly lied to David and Norma out of fear and self-preservation. I lied to them about where I was one Friday evening so I could enjoy a furlough from the cage I lived in at their house.

I was sixteen and really liked this boy, Jason. He had an olive green 1969 Mercury Cougar with the hideaway lights, and he was definitely giving off bad boy vibes. I was head over heels for him. My parents had a rule that I couldn't date anyone who didn't attend a Christian church. Jason went to a Christian church with his family, just not under their watchful eye at ours. He also went to a different school than I did, so I only got to see him every now and then. We had spent the summer together at Bible camp, and that's where we really got close.

He asked me to hang out that Friday night, so I asked my parents. Norma quickly said, "No!" which really shouldn't have surprised me, but it still didn't make sense. I had finished all my chores, the lawn was mowed, the dishes were clean and put away. It was one of the few times I was doing well in school and wasn't grounded. On top of that, I was holding down a job at Blockbuster. I reminded her that everything was done and that we were just going to watch a movie. She raised her voice, "I said no!"

I stormed off to my room, thinking, *This is so stupid. I never get to do anything.* There's no reason for this. I felt like a prisoner. David overheard the exchange and added, "You can't go because I already told Chip, your boss at Blockbuster, that you would work inventory that night." My whole body turned red with anger. "What? I already told Chip I was not going to work inventory. I did it the last two times!"

Working inventory meant that when we closed the store at eleven p.m., we had to take scanners and go through every video, every pickle, every package of candy and popcorn, and then wait for the manager to confirm that everything was accounted for. If there were any discrepancies, no one could leave until they were resolved. Sometimes I didn't get home until after three a.m.

I told David he had no business telling my boss when I could or couldn't work, and that I wasn't going. He told me I'd be grounded if I didn't go to work. I felt so powerless, so angry, so full of resentment. I called my manager, Brad, and told him I'd come in and stay until seven p.m., but like I had said before, I was NOT going to do inventory again. He needed to find someone else, or I was going to quit and not show up at all.

I called Jason and told him I was going to meet up with him after I got off work. I didn't tell my parents. I had been working so hard at school, at home, and at work, I felt I deserved a break. I deserved to have fun. I deserved some kind of freedom. And if they weren't going to give it to me, I was going to take it for myself.

As I was getting ready to leave for work, Norma told me they were going out for Chinese food that night and asked if I wanted them to bring me anything. I didn't even look at her; I just growled, "NO THANK YOU!" and left. I threw a change of clothes into my bag and headed to work, still fuming over the whole situation but also excited to see Jason later. It was a busy evening at Blockbuster, so the time flew by. Right before seven p.m., I told my manager I was going to clock out and leave. He asked again, "Are you sure you can't stay? We could really use your help." I snapped back, "Absolutely not. And the next time someone wants me to work, they can call me, not my parents. That better not ever happen again."

I clocked out, changed clothes, and made my way to Jason's home. We went out to grab takeout, brought it back to his place, and started a movie. Maybe an hour into the movie, Jason got a call from his parents.

"Is Melinda with you?" I could hear them ask on the other end.

He looked at me, confused, and answered, "Uh, yes, we are hanging out. Why?" His mother sounded upset. "Tell her she needs to call her parents now, and they are not happy. They know she is not at work like she is supposed to be."

I could feel my heart start to race. I knew the hell that was waiting for me at home.

Jason looked over again, still confused. "What is going on, Mel?" I told him what had happened with the inventory situation at work and how my parents wouldn't let me hang out with him. He was clearly frustrated.

"I get it, but you could get me in trouble now. You should've just told me the truth."

I apologized. He handed me his cell phone and said, "Here, call your parents."

With trembling fingers, I punched in 939-6075. "Hello, Mel, you have got fifteen minutes to get your ass home, young lady. We stopped by your work to drop off food, and you were not there. Your manager told us you went on a date after we said you were not allowed. You are in so much trouble," Norma yelled, then hung up the phone.

I started shaking and crying.

Jason asked, "Are you going to be okay?"

I just shook my head and said, "No, they are going to beat the crap out of me."

It didn't matter what I did; it felt as if I was never going to be treated any better or given any real freedom. I left Jason's house a little after ten p.m. and just drove. I was too afraid to go home. I needed space. I needed quiet. I needed to be angry without someone yelling at me. When I was just about to pull into the long driveway, red and blue bright, flashing lights belonging to the Bell County Sheriff's Department cruiser pulled close behind me.

Norma had called the police and reported me as a runaway. I was literally fifteen feet from turning onto the gravel road that led to our house. The officer walked up to my car and asked me to identify myself. I could hear him talking into his radio about a runaway.

"I didn't run away," I told him. "I just wasn't ready to come home." I said this sarcastically, maybe too sarcastically. "Can you just take me to jail? I'd rather go there than go home."

He wasn't amused at all, and who knows what Norma had told him over the phone.

He escorted me up the driveway to my parents' house. I felt as though I was walking up to the executioner stage, and the way Norma smacked my face and screamed at me repeatedly made me yearn for a guillotine; it would have been a lot quicker. As I walked up the porch steps, David extended his hands and said, "You lost your car!" The car that I saved for. The car that I worked for and paid for, my car. He took it away and sold it to my sister. I never saw the money.

Pamela knew how upset I was, but she never stood up for me. Never told them it was wrong. She just sat quietly, the way she always did, while they punished me and called it discipline. When I confronted her later, angry and heartbroken, all she said was, "Well, at least they sold it to me and not someone else." As if that made it okay; it didn't.

This happened in the summer of '99, and that next Saturday morning, David woke me up at 5:30 a.m. and told me to get my work clothes on. I got up and got ready just like he asked. Then he told me to eat breakfast, so I poured a bowl of cereal. After I ate, he told me to follow him outside. We walked to the southwest end of the property, and he handed me a weird cane-like tool to pick weeds. He said that for the next couple of weeks, I would be waking up at 5:30 a.m., eating breakfast, and then picking weeds. Norma would come get me when it was time for lunch. I'd come inside, eat, then go right back outside until David got home. Then I'd eat dinner, do the dishes, take a shower, and go to bed. This was my sentence.

One thing you should know, this property was not in some fancy home-owners' association, yard-of-the-month, Bermuda grass kind of place. There was barely any real grass at all. It was all weeds.

At lunchtime, Norma yelled for me from the porch, "Lunch!" I washed my hands, grabbed a Gatorade from the fridge, and sat down at the kitchen table. She placed a paper plate with a bologna sandwich in front of me and didn't say a word. She grabbed one of my hands to look at the blisters forming on my hands, let go, and still didn't say a word. I ate the sandwich, cleaned the table, threw my trash away, and went back outside into the 104-degree Texas summer heat. I stopped by the tool shed to grab a hoe, because the tool David had given me was tearing my hands apart. With the hoe, I could at least sweep across the yard and cut the weeds from the surface.

Those first few days were not fueled by bologna or peanut butter and jelly sandwiches. They were fueled by rage: deep, silent, concentrated rage. With every strike of that hoe, I let it out. I told myself over and over that I couldn't wait to turn eighteen so I could leave that place and never come back. I swore I would never treat anyone the way my family treated me. Even with everything they threw at me, they were never going to break my spirit. I was going to make something of my life. There had to be more than this.

Three or four days into my sentence, David came home from work a little early. He walked toward me with the weed-pulling cane tool in his hand. He threw it on the ground in front of me and asked coldly, "Why aren't you using the tool I gave you? Who told you to use the hoe?" I showed him my blistered, blood-covered hands and tried to explain that the cane tool was making them worse, and the hoe was easier to hold.

He pointed at a patch of yard I had just worked on and dropped to his knees where a few weeds were still visible. Then he stood up, drove the tip of that tool into the ground, twisted it, and pulled out a clump of roots. He walked over to the huge pile of weeds I had cut with the hoe, picked one up, held it out, and said, "You see, you didn't get the root, so it's gonna grow back!" Then he held up the weed he had just pulled. "See how deep the root was?" He looked at me and said, "You need to use the right tool so you get the weed out by the roots, or they will all grow back."

I told him the whole property was weeds. He snapped back, "Yeah, you got a lot of work to do!" He handed me a pair of gloves, which didn't help much with the blisters, and told me to get to work.

I walked back to the spot where I had started with the hoe and began finding the weeds I had already cut, using the cane tool to pull them up from the root. With every squeeze of that handle, it felt like shards of glass sinking deeper into my skin. But I swallowed my tears and clung to that anger like a shield.

Then David said, "Lying is like a weed. It's hard to destroy. And if you only get at it from the surface, it'll grow back. You gotta use the right tools and pull it from its roots. That's why you're out here, so do it right!" He turned around and walked back into the house.

That night, I didn't eat dinner. I stayed out there, pulling weeds with that tool well past sundown. Finally, Norma came outside, feigning concern and said, "It's getting late. Go inside and take a shower, and I'll get you something for your blisters." By that time, her concern was much too late.

As the sky darkened and my hands burned, something inside me shifted. I wasn't just pulling weeds anymore: I was wrestling with the kind of hurt that sinks deep, the kind that makes you question everything you're supposed to believe about love, forgiveness, and God. That yard became more than a punishment; it became a place where faith and my reality collided.

Out there in that yard, I wondered how Jesus could look at the very people who beat Him, spit on Him, nailed Him to a cross, and still beg God to forgive them. How He could still love them. How He could see past all their brokenness. I couldn't do that at sixteen, and I still struggle to do it as an adult.

But when I manage to extend grace, even in small ways, I have to face something uncomfortable: I'm not separate from the people who hurt me; I'm one of them. I've had my own selfish moments, my own anger, my own blind spots. I've needed forgiveness more times than I can count. I've carried my own pain, regret, guilt, and shame. And I've needed freedom from all of it just as much as anyone else.

Maybe that's why I see kids differently now, kids who lie, who mess up, who act out. I recognize the fear behind their behavior, the way consequences feel bigger than their capacity, the way silence can swallow your voice. I understand what it's like to tell a lie not to deceive but because the truth doesn't feel safe. I understand the pressure that makes your chest tight and your choices small. I understand wanting freedom so badly, you'll take it any way you can.

Lying isn't always about dishonesty; sometimes it's about survival. That's the part no one explained to me then. And maybe that's what David was trying to get at with all his talk about roots, how if you don't deal with what's underneath, the same patterns keep growing back. What I know now is this: If someone is willing to dig a little deeper, be patient a little longer, and show up with steady love, healing becomes possible. Not just for the kid who lied, but for the adult who learned to lie because she thought it was the only way to stay safe.

CHAPTER 5

Be All That You Can Be

LIFE IN THAT house became increasingly strained as time went on. I constantly begged my sister Pamela to come get me, as she had moved out by then. I just wanted to live with her, to escape the tension, the volatility, and the emotional toll. Pamela had worked hard to graduate early so she could leave, and when she did, I felt abandoned by the one steady person who had always been there.

In the middle of my senior year of high school, I finally left David and Norma's home. It had gotten so bad there that even my sister couldn't turn a blind eye to it anymore. She showed up and told David that she was picking me up to take me with her. He yelled and screamed at her for interfering, and I will never forget what she yelled back at both of them: "She is no longer your problem, so just let her go." Her relationship with them was strained for quite a bit because of it, but they were never angry with her for too long.

And so, I moved in with my sister and her roommate for several months, but my sister was done raising me. The destructive tailspin I was slipping into was not her responsibility; she was trying to find her own way at the same time. I was ditching class and smoking weed with friends. The school called David and Norma, and they called Pamela. She warned me that if I didn't stop, I'd get kicked out of her place. But I was far beyond her or anyone's threats. I continued to self-destruct and soon, she kicked me out.

From there, I went to live with Janelle, a kind woman from our church who wanted to help, and maybe needed company, too. But I wasn't ready for anyone's help, nor was I willing to accept control in any form. She tried to give me curfews and rules; looking back now, they were entirely reasonable. She intended to protect and save me. But I resisted hard. It was the first time I was free from the abuse, control, and cage David and Norma kept me in, and I pushed back against anything that even smelled like their rules.

A couple of months before high school graduation, my guidance counselor called me in. I was missing too many days and too many assignments to graduate. My heart sank. I shouldn't have been surprised, but I was scared. I spoke with my teachers, who had no idea what was going on in my life, and I begged for a chance to make things right. In a meeting with school administrators and teachers, I told them everything. I explained that I needed to graduate so I could join the military and have some kind of future.

In a perfect example of unmerited grace, Mrs. Potts, my school guidance counselor, advocated for me and worked out a plan for me to make up my missed hours and assignments. In those final two months, I checked in with her daily, and I worked incredibly hard to catch up, and in May of 2001, I walked across the stage and graduated high school on time.

Not long after graduation, I enlisted in the Army. If it seems extreme to say I joined the military just to get away, maybe that speaks to how difficult things had become. I wasn't chasing some patriotic dream; I was seeking safety, and the Army became my way out. I enlisted in a world designed to train people for war, not because I wanted to fight one overseas but because I was desperate to escape the war I couldn't fight inside my own home or within myself.

I had spent years trying to be heard. My defiance, my talking back, none of it was rebellion for rebellion's sake. It was a scream into the void, an unrelenting plea to be seen and protected. No one came; no one stepped in. So, I became what I needed. I turned myself into the very protector I had longed for. The Army didn't just represent escape: it represented power, control, and survival. It was the armor I chose to wear after years of being left exposed, the only place I could think of that offered structure, stability, and the promise of something different. Something stronger. Something safer.

As an imaginative little girl, I dreamt of becoming an astronaut and boldly going where no man has gone before. I attended an elementary school in Washington state named after astronaut Dick Scobee, and everything about the school revolved around space exploration. I loved it. That experience sparked a fascination with the stars and a yearning for exploration I still carry with me today.

When I joined the Army, I intended to participate in the High School-to-Flight School program. I might not have been on track to become an astronaut, but I thought perhaps I could still fly free in the skies. That was my dream, at least, until I met the smooth-talking, quota-driven Army recruiter.

Thanks to my high General Technical (GT) score on the Armed Services Vocational Aptitude Battery (ASVAB) exam, I was a perfect fit for a hard-to-fill role, Army counterintelligence special agent (97B). The GT portion of the exam measures cognitive skills, problem-solving, and logical thinking, acting as a gateway for advanced technical, intelligence and leadership positions. He asked me if I liked James Bond movies; of course, my answer was yes. And let the record show the best James Bond of all time is, without a doubt, Sir Sean Connery.

The recruiter played a training film that showcased all the flash and appeal of being a Special Agent 97B: civilian clothes, excitement, prestige, and the quiet honor of being the unsung hero behind the scenes. It worked. I signed the papers.

To my surprise, I initially enjoyed basic training. I loved the camaraderie, the structure, the physical challenge, and the opportunity to lead. It was a surprising fit for me, and I did well. There was an unspoken saying: If you could shoot, move, and communicate, you could get away with murder. For me, it wasn't about getting away with anything. For the first time, I felt seen as a strong, capable, and competent person. It gave me the validation and acceptance I had craved for so long. Until it didn't.

I earned the respect of the cadre and drill sergeants because I worked hard and showed promise as a leader. They were "cool" with me, until they weren't. In basic training, we had a strict battle buddy system. You never went anywhere alone, especially around a drill sergeant. If you were caught alone, it meant immediate pushups. And not just for you but for the poor soldier who happened to be nearby. "Front-leaning rest position, move!"

One night, during our CQ (Charge of Quarters) duty, a rotating security assignment for the barracks, my battle buddy and I ran into Drill Sergeant Salas. He was one of the "cool" ones: funny, approachable, someone who treated us like adults. We stopped in the hallway to give our report. When we mentioned we were heading to the laundry room to move our clothes to the dryer, he told my battle buddy to go ahead; he'd wait with me. We exchanged uneasy glances. The rules were clear: Never be alone. But he was a drill sergeant, and he said it was fine. So, she left.

Drill Sergeant Salas suggested we walk the perimeter while we waited. As we moved down a dim hallway, everything changed. Without warning, he grabbed me and slammed me against the cold, concrete wall. My head hit hard. I felt disoriented, dizzy. He pressed his body into mine, kissed me, bit at my face and neck. His hands began to roam under my shirt, interrupted only by the returning footsteps of my battle buddy

He turned to me, shoved his knife-hand in my face, and said, "If you tell anyone, no one will believe you. You'll be kicked out of the Army." When my battle buddy rounded the corner, she looked confused. She heard him yelling at me and saw the tension. When he walked away, she asked, "What did you do? Please don't get us in trouble." I swallowed the lump in my throat. I swallowed the truth. For days, Salas was no longer the friendly, supportive sergeant. He was cruel, especially to me. I was terrified.

Eventually, I found the courage to speak up. I waited until a female drill sergeant was on duty and told her everything.

I was immediately moved to another training unit, where I was treated like a problem. As if I had caused something, again. That moment reinforced a message I had already started to believe: My body was a liability, and the truth didn't protect me. I couldn't trust the people who were supposed to protect and lead me. I was lost.

Later, I learned that after I came forward, several other women reported similar experiences. Salas was court-martialed, reduced in rank, and reassigned to the infantry, where, according to his command, he could, "flourish in an environment without the distraction of women." It's hard to describe what it feels like to hear something like that, as if our presence as women was the problem. Not his abuse of power. Not the trauma he caused. Just our existence. As if by removing women from his line of sight, the danger would simply dissolve. No accountability. Just relocation. Reframing. Redirection.

I wish I could tell you that reporting Drill Sergeant Salas made things better. That it was the last time. But it wasn't. I experienced sexual assault or harassment at every single duty station I was assigned to in nearly ten years of service. Each time, it came from someone in leadership. Someone charged with my safety and well-being.

This is a deep wound in our military, a culture that too often fails to protect the very people who sacrifice everything to serve. Not all leaders are like that, but far too many are. And the scars they left made it nearly impossible for me to trust not just leaders but men in general for most of my life.

I didn't run away to the Army only to serve. I ran to escape the war inside my home and the chaos inside myself. I chose a life where people were trained to go to war because it felt safer than the war I had already survived. But the truth was the war never ended. The battlefield simply changed.

I completed training and was assigned my first duty station in Wiesbaden, Germany, in 2002. The glamorous image of badge-flashing and civilian clothes quickly gave way to the reality of ruck marches, motor pool Mondays, and training exercises in snow up to our knees. As soldiers often say, "It was the best of times, it was the worst of times."

The hell we endured was made bearable because we didn't endure it alone. I formed strong friendships with people from all over the world, bonds that, thanks to social media, have lasted decades later. Those friendships were a lifeline.

But not all relationships in that chapter were healthy. I was finally an adult, managing my own money (poorly), with the freedom I'd never known; I wasn't ready for it. The teenage years that should have taught me responsibility and resilience were stifled by control and fear. So, I learned those lessons the hard way as an adult. And the consequences were real. Promiscuity. Financial instability. Alcohol abuse. I fell into a pit of patterns that I didn't know how to break. I let men assign me my worth one moment at a time, and I let the echoes of abandonment and rejection scream loudest in my twenties than ever before.

But even in the darkest places, there were moments of light. I was assigned to the 1st Armored Division, and we had deployed to Iraq for an eight-month rotation. As its end approached, I eagerly anticipated returning home and attending my sister's wedding in Texas. She had found a good man, patient with her pain. He offered the kind of love that heals. I was overjoyed to celebrate that moment with her. After those hot, long, and frightening eight months, we started preparing to redeploy to Germany. Everything was packed: gear, equipment, vehicles. We lined up on the tarmac ready to board the plane. Then came the announcement—no one was leaving. Our orders had changed. We were staying for at least another six months. The unit that was supposed to replace us, 1st Cavalry Division, wasn't trained or equipped for the level of conflict unfolding in Baghdad. The city was under near-constant attack, with bombings, roadside mortars, ambushes, and chaos. We were still needed, and so we were ordered to remain. I was furious. But there were no tears; it was too hot to cry. Literally. That summer, temperatures reached 140 degrees Fahrenheit. I would miss my sister's wedding, and there was nothing I could do.

Back at BIAP (Baghdad International Airport), I pulled six hours of guard duty in blistering heat. I was exhausted and emotionally frayed. All I wanted was to call my sister, but my NCOIC had other plans. He grabbed me after shift and ordered me to push slides for the general's daily briefing. I protested that I hadn't slept in over twenty-four hours. He didn't care:

some things needed to get done, and I was an asset, a cog in the machine, nothing more.

That day, I had my first encounter with our new division commander, Major General Martin Dempsey. I had briefed our previous commander General Sanchez, and he was terrifying with his awkward and demanding, "So what?" questions. During this particularly significant activity update briefing, one officer proposed recruiting the foreign national workers (Iraqi civilians) who cleaned our port-a-potties as intel sources. I couldn't hide my disbelief. I thought I muttered under my breath, but clearly it was louder than I realized. Everyone turned to glare at me except Gen. Dempsey. He looked at me curiously.

"Sergeant Jackson," he said. "Is there something you'd like to add?"

Panicked, I stood at attention and replied, "Negative, sir, not a thing."

He stood up from his chair. "No, I think there is. That was a strong reaction. Speak your mind."

My Analysis Control Element (ACE) Chief whispered behind me, "Jackson, keep your mouth shut." I was known to have an outspoken opinion, mostly passive-aggressive sarcasm, and he was afraid I was about to say something that would embarrass him. But my mouth often engaged more quickly than my brain, and it was too late for warnings.

With a boldness that was fueled more by fear than anything, I explained why the suggestion was dangerous. We would be unintentionally incentivizing misinformation. Already, desperate locals fabricated stories to earn money from different units, creating circular reporting that looked valid but wasn't. Soldiers were being sent into ambushes based on lies. It was careless; it was deadly.

The room was silent. I was certain I'd just destroyed my career. Then Gen. Dempsey did something unthinkable: He walked over to me, ushered me to his seat at the head of the table, then moved over to where I was sitting and clicked the slides himself and said, "Let's hear from someone who knows what they're talking about." He was talking about needing to hear from me. I was terrified but also deeply validated. He didn't just give me a voice. He trusted it.

Afterward, he took an interest in my career. He pulled strings to get me reassigned to the elite 902nd Military Intelligence Group at Fort Meade, Maryland, instead of another tactical unit in Fort Drum, New York, which was soon to deploy and take me right back to Iraq. He remains one of the wisest leaders I've ever encountered. Later, he became chairman of the Joint Chiefs of Staff under President Barack Obama, and I couldn't have been prouder to have served under him.

He even sent a handwritten letter to David, praising me, thanking him for raising such a strong and capable soldier. He addressed me by name; it meant the world. In a place where I had so often been overlooked, silenced, or harmed, someone saw me. Really saw me. And it reminded me that even in war, especially in war, there is still room for honor, truth, and dignity. And maybe for the first time, I started to believe there was room for me, too.

CHAPTER 6

Home Sweet Home

I T WAS MY twenty-second birthday, and for the first time in a long time, something in me felt light. I'd spent my last birthday in Iraq, and now, finally, we were leaving a war that had taken too many lives and damaged the rest of us in ways some of us wouldn't understand until much later. And this time, I wasn't just leaving a battlefield. I was leaving with something I hadn't carried in years: hope.

With a quick phone call to the INSCOM Commander, Gen. Dempsey changed the trajectory of my career and life. I was heading back to Germany with my unit, then going on leave before starting a new assignment at Fort Meade, Maryland. A new assignment. A new chapter. A chance to breathe.

And part of me, maybe the most wounded part, hoped that everything I had endured and survived would mean something to David and Norma. That maybe they'd finally see me. Maybe they'd be proud. Maybe the uniform, the war, the sacrifice would shift something in the way they looked at me.

But hope is fragile. And mine didn't survive the landing.

I stepped into Dallas/Fort Worth International Airport to rows of strangers cheering, waving flags, reaching out with tears in their eyes.

They didn't know my name, but they saw me. They honored me. For a moment, I felt held.

David, Norma, and my stepbrother met me later for dinner. No signs. No welcome. No real questions. Just polite conversation wrapped around an emptiness I knew too well. David seemed irritated by the attention we'd received at the airport.

"You all are treated like heroes," he said, almost bitter. "When I came back from Vietnam, they treated us like murderers."

The way he said *heroes* lodged itself in me. Like he couldn't stand the thought of anyone praising me for anything. That moment stayed with me.

I had imagined a homecoming, something soft, something steady, something that felt like belonging. What I got was the same old truth I had been trying to outrun: time, distance, and even war can't change some people. They can't change the way they see you. Or the way they don't. I wanted to feel like I was coming home. But the minute my boots hit Texas soil, something in my chest tightened: sharp, hollow, familiar. This wasn't home. Not anymore. Maybe it never had been.

Still, I made the most of those weeks. I spent time with old friends from high school. I visited with my sister, her husband, and his family, people who had always welcomed me, without question or hesitation.

I was heartbroken that I missed my sister's wedding. I was so happy for her, and I know it wasn't reasonable to expect them to postpone it for me, but I still wished I could've been there. Pamela and I had talked about being each other's bridesmaids since we were little girls, back when we believed in fairy tales and handsome princes and the kind of happily-ever-afters that felt simple and certain.

Her wedding was a reminder that the world kept spinning without me while I was waking up every day on the other side of it, wondering if it would be my last.

Still, watching from a distance, something tender stirred in me, a quiet hope that maybe one day I could find what she had found. The love. The belonging. The sense of being chosen. The way her husband's family embraced her made me feel warm and wistful all at once. I wanted what that represented: safety, belonging, a place to be fully known and still fully loved.

By then, I had saved quite a bit of money. Eighteen months of deployment with no bills and nowhere to spend meant I came home with more in my bank account than I'd ever seen. But no one had ever taught me how to manage money or plan for the future, so I did what any twenty-two-year-old returning from war with a pocket full of deployment pay and a love for fast cars would do. I bought a brand-new 2004 Mazda Rx-8.

It wasn't just a car. It was the first thing in my life that felt like mine. Something fast enough to outrun the heaviness I'd been carrying. Something loud enough to drown out everything I didn't know how to say. After years of living under other people's orders, expectations, and control, sliding into that driver's seat felt like freedom. Like choosing myself for the first time. Like claiming something no one could take from me.

I packed up the back seat with everything I owned that hadn't been shipped from Germany. I set the GPS to Fort Meade, Maryland, and with music playing and windows down, I drove cross-country. I didn't know what awaited me on the other end. But for the first time in a long time, I felt forward motion. And maybe that was enough to call it home.

The communication with my new NCOIC at Fort Meade was not what I expected, especially not from someone in a leadership position at the 902d Military Intelligence Group. From the outside, 902d was the Army Intelligence Community's crème de la crème. A high-speed, high-stakes unit supporting national-level collection efforts. Real-world missions. Global impact. To be assigned there was an honor. I was thrilled; I had earned it. I arrived with a sense of pride, hope, and expectation.

But disappointment hit me hard. My NCOIC, who should have set the standard, met me with thinly veiled pretension. She was on a permanent profile for a "back injury" that excused her from doing PT with the unit, yet she openly bragged about powerlifting outside of duty hours. Her uniform looked strained and sloppy, because she didn't carry herself with the discipline the uniform demanded. She had never deployed, never investigated, never led soldiers in conditions that tested them. And yet she was the one in charge. What bothered me was the contradiction. The double standard. The absence of the professionalism we were trained to live by.

To me, she wasn't a leader; she was a clerk with rank. And underneath the paperwork and procedures, she was deeply insecure. I felt it immediately: in her posture, in her clipped tone, in the way she tried to assert authority without ever demonstrating it. From day one, I could tell I made her uncomfortable, and in an environment like ours, discomfort quickly turns into threat.

She never tried to mentor me. Never offered guidance. Instead, she quietly worked to limit me: blocking opportunities, withholding advanced training, and keeping me tucked away in the orderly room of headquarters company, where potential went unnoticed and ambition went to die.

But thankfully, I wasn't alone. There were other leaders in the unit, ones with more rank and better judgment, who saw my potential and gave me a shot; that only fueled her resentment further. She hated that I went around her to get what other agents were receiving freely. She hated that her authority wasn't enough to bury me. But what she didn't realize was this: I had survived far worse than her before.

Still, if I'm honest, I didn't make it easy on myself. The girl who had once been silenced without defense or dignity had grown into a woman who felt injustice in her bones. Life had trained me to read motive, sense threat, and protect myself before anyone else could take that choice from me. And when my suspicions about her proved right, it didn't ease anything; it hardened what was already fragile inside me. It reinforced the belief I'd carried for years: that leaders weren't safe. But the Army, especially a unit like the 902d, required a different kind of discipline. A long game. A closed mouth. Knowing when to speak and when to wait. I hadn't learned that yet.

I had a sharp tongue and a wounded heart, and the echoes of my trauma leaked through both. I wasn't just reacting to her; I was reacting to every buried moment of injustice that had come before her. And in my fight to be heard, I didn't realize I was losing ground I'd need later. I wanted to be sharp. Untouchable. The kind of soldier no one would question. But the cracks in my armor were there, and eventually, they showed.

Alcohol was a vice I quickly overcame once I moved out of the environment in Europe that promoted drinking and partying. One brutal bout of alcohol poisoning in Germany was enough to scare me straight.

To this day, I'll have a drink now and then, but no more than one. I don't like losing control. I don't like who I become under the influence. And I've learned to listen to that discomfort. But where alcohol lost its grip, something else took hold: spending. Shopping became my escape, my addiction. And it would take years before I could even admit how deep it ran. It sounds harmless, but for me, it was as destructive as any substance. Maybe even more.

Money became my camouflage. Designer suits. Statement shoes. Perfectly matched accessories. Clothing was just one way I learned to curate an image, an illusion of control, success, and invulnerability. In the world of military intelligence, perception was reality. And I was fluent in the language of illusion. I knew how to wear the right smile. How to keep my tone gentle. How to come across as polished, trustworthy, and with just the right amount of vulnerability. I could charm a room. Build rapport with anyone. Gain anyone's trust.

But I didn't handle that power with the care it deserved. I was still learning who I was beneath the performance. The truth is my financial recklessness eventually caught up with me. Sometimes it even spilled into my professional life, tarnishing the reputation I had worked so hard to build. And in my line of work, reputation wasn't just a bonus—it was everything.

With my level of responsibility and access, the security clearance, the trust, the position, there was no room for personal liabilities. No cracks in the story. No visible flaws. Anything that could be used against you would be. Others were better at hiding their vices. Their scars. Their humanity. Mine sometimes showed.

But by God's grace and the presence of real leadership, I wasn't discarded. I was challenged. I was given space to own my mistakes and rise through them. Leaders like 1st Sergeant Thomas Whittington and Captain Sam Smith didn't just see my faults: they saw my potential. They saw the person behind the missteps. And they gave me the one thing I had rarely been offered in life, a chance to grow. I paid for my mistakes, but I wasn't disqualified by them.

And on the other side of that growth came something incredible. I was offered a coveted training slot at the Joint Counterintelligence Training Academy's Advanced Agents Course, immediately after completing the Counterintelligence Force Protection Source Operations (CFSO) course. My boss called the morning I finished CFSO. "Don't check out of your hotel," he said. "You're starting surveillance training on Monday." I was stunned and exhilarated.

This was it. This was the stuff recruiters told wide-eyed 97B James Bond hopefuls about in their earliest days. This was the real work, the high-level training that opened doors across the intelligence world. And somehow, despite everything, I was walking through one of them.

CHAPTER 7

Watch Out Boys

I 'LL NOT WRITE much in this memoir about the men I dated in this chapter. There were a lot of them, but only a few that lasted. I never had a model for what a healthy relationship looked like. Norma was David's fifth wife. My mother floated in and out of relationships as they benefited her. Love was never the core of any of it, only survival, security, and convenience, so I didn't know any other way to be.

I sought companionship and intimacy in ways that suited the moment, ways that let me disappear for a little while into something that felt like connection. Moments of passion became my escape. They numbed the pain, the confusion, the shame I carried like a shadow in my chest. There were good men. And there were bad men. But either way, when they got too close, when I approached that invisible line of real vulnerability, I cut the cord. Every time.

I never allowed myself to be fully known. Not by any man. And barely by a handful of friends. The truth of who I was felt too heavy. Too ugly. If I could suppress it enough, I could even forget who I was. But sometimes, a person shows up who gently and quietly peels back your armor, without your permission, and before you're ready. That's what Timothy did.

It was the weekend after I graduated from the CFSO course, and I was on my way back to the schoolhouse to start the Advanced Agents Course. I sped into the corner parking lot of JCITA, music up, dark-tinted windows, and practically drifted into the empty spot next to a sleek, black 1992 Mustang 5.0 convertible. It was the fox-body style, the kind only a true car enthusiast could appreciate. And it looked just like the one in Aerosmith's *Crazy* video. You know the one, Alicia Silverstone and Liv Tyler tearing down the Pacific Coast Highway with the top down, every guy in the nineties losing their minds. It was iconic. And I wanted to park next to it, not just for convenience but for admiration. I wanted whoever drove that Mustang to see my RX-8 and feel the same kind of appreciation I felt for their car.

I was driving too fast to see Timothy clearly, but he was there, leaning casually on the other side of the Mustang with a couple of friends, waiting for class to start. My tires squealed a little too close for comfort. I could feel the air shift. They stiffened. Glaring. Disapproving. I heard one of them mutter, "Who the hell is this?"

Then I stepped out. Fitted pencil skirt. Long, olive-skin legs. Sky-high heels. A floral blouse and cardigan, conservative but hugging my frame in all the right places. Shoulder-length, golden-brown hair. Big dark eyes. A bright white smile. Their jaws hit the pavement. I met his eyes.

"Sorry about that," I said gently. "Didn't realize I got that close. I can move over if you want."

He blinked. Composed himself. "Yeah," he said, trying to sound annoyed. "That was a little nuts. But you're fine. No need to move."

I smiled. "See you around." I didn't know if he'd be in my course. JCITA had several courses running at once, and this could've been the first and last time I ever saw him. But the way he looked at me, that flash of something between challenge and curiosity, I had a feeling I'd be seeing him again.

Inside the classroom, heads turned. Curious eyes followed me as I made my way to my seat. This wasn't just another course. And these weren't just students. This was Detachment 13, the Surveillance and Operational Support unit for the 902d. These were the cool guys doing the cool guy intel stuff. I would love to tell you more about that world. But, you know, then I'd have to kill you.

The course was structured in three progressive phases: Operational

Support, Surveillance, and Offensive Counterintelligence Operations. It was designed to be grueling, intense, and as close to the real thing as you could get. And it was taught in a cohort model, meaning everyone in my class had already been through most of it together. They knew one another. They had trained together. Proven themselves to one another. I was the outsider, and I had my work cut out for me.

The course lasted a month, with the first week spent entirely in the classroom. We had to learn a specialized syntax, a coded language used to communicate with the surveillance team about who we were, where the target was headed, and what they were doing. It was like learning a completely new language, and every part of it was built on an advanced understanding of urban land navigation.

Now, let me set the bar exactly where it needs to be. I came from a real Army tactical environment. If you dropped me out of a helicopter into the forest with nothing but a compass, a protractor, a map, and a set of grid coordinates, I could find the Holy Grail and meet you at the rendezvous point on time. But drop me onto I-395 or I-95 in Washington D.C. traffic, and I was lost and on the verge of a full-blown panic attack. In this course, we weren't allowed to use our vehicles or GPS. We were issued rental cars, no nav systems, no shortcuts. Just paper maps, colored dot stickers, and our ability to memorize and communicate terrain. I was completely handicapped.

The rest of the class had already been practicing and preparing for this for weeks; I hadn't. I didn't know the language. I didn't love the endless dot-sticking onto oversized maps. I didn't connect with the material. And being honest, I didn't give it the effort it needed, and it showed.

That first week of field practice, radio calls, finger-mapping, surveillance maneuvers, I was terrible. To make things worse, there was always something wrong with my coms or the vehicle or whatever else the universe could throw at me to remind me, and everyone else, that I didn't belong there. And truthfully, I agreed. But my pride wouldn't let me quit.

My instructor encouraged me to spend extra time after class practicing call-outs, refining my syntax. I knew he was right. But I hated the work, and I certainly didn't want to spend the little free time I had doing more of it until I couldn't avoid it anymore. It was obvious; I needed help. And who offered to help me? None other than Mr. Magellan himself, Timothy. If I was the weakest link in the chain, he was the strongest.

Every week, the course selected a "Sierra Charlie," a surveillance chief, based on merit and performance. I was never picked, and no one was surprised. Timothy, though? He was picked several times. He was a natural. Where I would get overwhelmed and frazzled trying to track a target, report position, and manage the chaos, he stayed calm. Cool. Collected. He always seemed to know exactly what to do.

He offered to help me after class, and we'd spend hours driving through the city. He'd pick a random car to follow, and I'd practice calling out its position, movements, and behavior as if we were on a real op.

At first, I was convinced he'd been voluntold, but he never treated it like an obligation. He was patient. Kind. Honest about how much help I needed, but never unkind in saying so. He gave his time and attention without expecting anything in return; that alone made him different. I hadn't known many people like that. Certainly not many men.

In those hours together, we got to know each other. Or at least, I got to know him. He only got to see the version of me I allowed, the acceptable pieces, the polished parts. And like I had done so many times before, I studied what he wanted and became her. Through charm and illusion, I gave him a sliver of truth wrapped in layers of performance and illusion.

With his help, I started doing better in class. But the truth was I was still too far behind the curve to catch up. I made the kinds of mistakes people usually made in the first week. Everyone else had moved on. Then came the final exercise. One last chance.

I was paired with Kara, another student, on "bumper." We were parked near the target's last known location, watching and waiting to see where he would go. It was the kind of assignment that required sharp attention, quick communication, and absolute precision. The target vehicle was a dark green, late 1990s Dodge Caravan.

S-codes and urban navigation? I was shaky. But cars? Cars I knew. There were multiple teams on bumper duty, and within minutes, someone radioed in: "7777, X-ray 1 navigating the cup, straight at blue 1 3, 9 1 moon." That was the signal: target identified; movement confirmed. The chase was on. The rest of the team called out where they were in the follow, and Kara and I stayed behind to join last.

But something didn't feel right. The plate number they called out didn't match what we had noted earlier. I turned to Kara. "I don't think they're following the right van," I said.

She shook her head. "They're on track."

I asked her to double-check the plate number they'd called in. When she did, it didn't match what we had. I pressed again. "Check your notes."

Reluctantly, she did. And there it was, driving right in front of us, the green Dodge Caravan with the correct plates. I discreetly grabbed her arm below the dash. "That's it. That's the target. They're following the wrong one."

She started the car and slowly pulled out to follow. Excitement surged through me. I grabbed the radio and yelled, "7777. . . ."

Everyone went quiet. I reported that the team was tracking the wrong vehicle and that Kara and I were now following the correct one.

The response? Dismissive. Skeptical. "Get off the radio."

No one believed me. My reputation had followed me into that moment, but I was right this time. The instructors broke in to confirm: The rest of the team had been following the wrong vehicle north for twenty-five minutes.

It should have been my redemption. My moment. But instead, it became a race. We had the target, but we were alone, moving fast down the highway, and the rest of the team had to catch up. I tried to direct them, but I got turned around. They couldn't find us. We were not on the road where I was sending the rest of the team. Eventually, another teammate found us, and they took over the follow.

I'd been bold. I'd been right. But I'd also been reckless. I passed the course, but barely. And I didn't receive a recommendation to join the surveillance team. That evaluation was fair.

At the end of each week, they handed out awards for notable students. At graduation, I received a special one of my own: a stuffed dead squirrel wearing a trench coat, fedora, dark sunglasses, and a walking stick. The engraving on the base read, "Even blind squirrels can get nuts!" It was fitting, both hilarious and painfully accurate. A lighthearted nod to how wildly out of my depth I had been in surveillance. But what I didn't gain in skill, I gained in something else. Timothy and I started something new when the course ended.

We graduated just before Christmas. I went home to Texas to be with my sister. He headed to California to see his family. We talked every day. He even stayed on the phone with me for hours as I made the long drive from Maryland to Texas. It was the first real relationship I had ever been in. He was good to me. Attentive. Patient. Until he wasn't.

I wish I could keep your sympathy here. I wish I could tell you that I found a man who turned out just like David, kind and gentle in the beginning, then unexpectedly cruel and violent. But that wouldn't be the truth. Timothy wasn't the villain of this story; I was.

Yes, he changed. He became distant at times, cold, someone I didn't recognize. But the man he became was shaped, in part, by the fractures I brought into the marriage. Like David once loved my mother more than life itself, Timothy loved me with a kind of devotion I didn't know how to receive. I was his world. And he treated me like I was the most precious thing in it.

But long before we ever said "I do," I knew the truth I couldn't admit out loud: he couldn't truly ever love me because he didn't fully know me. He knew the version of me I had crafted for him, the polished mirage, the girl who said and did all the right things, who played the role of the woman he wanted. Illusions can hold for a while, but they always crack.

What I didn't understand then was **why** I kept creating illusions in the first place. Why I kept performing, pretending, pleasing. Why I reached for attention in ways that left me emptier. Why I ran to the arms of men I didn't care about rather than face the ache inside me.

It took me years to see it, but the pattern wasn't random. It was hunger. A deep, spiritual hunger I didn't have words for yet. That's where John 6 comes in, not as a sermon but as a mirror.

Jesus feeds a crowd of thousands with almost nothing, bread and fish, and instead of seeing the miracle, the people come back wanting more.

Not because they're greedy. Because they're starving for something they can't name. Jesus calls it out gently: "You're not looking for bread. You're looking for life."

For the first time, I realized that promiscuity works the same way. On the surface, it looks like desire, lust, recklessness. But underneath, it's often a soul-level ache, a longing to be chosen, to be held, to be wanted without conditions. When you grow up without protection or, worse, with harm, something in you starts asking the same silent question over and over:

Will anyone stay? Will anyone pick me? Am I worth keeping?

And when the answer feels like "no," your body learns behaviors your soul never agreed to.

It isn't about sex. Not really. It's about survival. Control. Validation. Numbing the parts of you that feel too heavy to carry sober. I didn't understand that then. I only knew how to run. How to hide. How to reach for the wrong things because the right things felt impossible.

Like the crowd in John 6, I kept going back for the thing that filled me for a moment but left me hollow again. I didn't need another man. I needed a place to rest. A place to feel safe. To be seen without performing. To be loved without earning it. What I was starving for was real connection, belonging, and a love that didn't disappear when I took the mask off.

CHAPTER 8

The Scar That Mirrors My Mother

I USED TO tell myself I was nothing like my mother. Yet I found myself carrying the echoes of both my parents, repeating the very behaviors I swore I never would.

By the first year of our relationship, Timothy and I had moved in together. However, he had already begun to suspect I was unfaithful. Anytime I traveled for work, his suspicions flared. Interrogations followed. Where were you? Why didn't you answer your phone? Who were you with? And his instincts weren't wrong.

Almost every time I was away for an extended period, I found comfort somewhere else. It wasn't because I was searching for love. It was because I was unconsciously sabotaging something I already knew wouldn't last. But I was too afraid to let him go and even more afraid to tell the truth. So, I kept lying. I manipulated reality. I built a story out of smoke and shadows and hoped it would hold.

And I think, on some level, he knew. Timothy's an intelligent man; he had to sense the shift. Maybe he couldn't admit it to himself. Or maybe his love had slowly morphed into something else, something closer to control. Just like David refused to let my mother go, Timothy didn't want to let me go either.

He rarely shared his feelings unless they came out as anger or disappointment. He was often aloof, detached. And while I won't use that to justify my betrayal, I owe it to myself to be honest. Timothy was not a safe place for me.

He loved me. He gave. He tried. But there was always an air of quiet condescension that lingered between us, especially when it came to me. I remember the first time he brought me to California to meet his family. I adored his father, Paul, and his stepfather, Tom. They were warm, welcoming, and kind. But his mother and brothers? If I'm being completely transparent, they were pretentious. Not in the way wealth sometimes is, but in that particular *LA vibe,* where image mattered more than substance. His brothers worked at high-end restaurants in the city, and his mother was a nanny for a wealthy doctor, which seemed to give them this air of importance.

They lived in a modest farming town outside of Thousand Oaks but carried themselves like they were part of the Hollywood elite. It wasn't about what they had; it was about who they were trying to be. And somehow, I never quite measured up.

His mother prepared a beautiful dinner for us one night, an incredible pork loin with cranberry reduction. I'd never tasted anything so elegant outside of a restaurant. I was genuinely impressed and probably went overboard with the compliments. I hovered near the kitchen, curious and eager to learn. I didn't grow up learning to cook. I had a few dishes I could make, but Timothy was the cook in our relationship.

As we sat down to eat, I took a bite and, without thinking, said, "Wow, my dad would love this; he loves pork chops." The room went silent. They all looked at me as if I was a hillbilly just dropped out of the sky into Beverly Hills by mistake. And Timothy, smirking in front of everyone, said, "Uh, yeah … this isn't pork chops. Not sure your dad would like this." And they laughed.

That was the first time I felt dismissed by him, humiliated, like he was trying to prove something to them, like he had brought home charity, and I should be grateful to dine at their table. In that moment, something cracked. Not just between us, but inside me. I wasn't just embarrassed. I was nine years old again, sitting on the floor while adults whispered about how I talked too much, ate too fast, and didn't belong. I had worked so hard to become someone worthy of the room. But I remained the outsider. Still the one being laughed at for not knowing the difference between pork chops and pork loin. Still the girl no one protected.

Throughout that trip, it happened more than once. Little digs. Passive snickers. And when his mother made a comment about how disappointed she was that Timothy had joined the Army, because he went to college and was "too good" for it, I snapped.

"Well," I said, "he's in the Army. And so am I. And neither of us is too good for any of it."

I think she knew then that I saw through her carefully curated facade of class and refinement. I loved Tom, Timothy's stepfather, and enjoyed his company. I really did. But once again, I found myself at a table where I didn't belong.

Shortly after that trip, while Timothy and I were still dating, the Army sent me on a temporary assignment to Kuwait for real-world source operations. Another birthday in the Middle East. Another year that would have passed without notice until I checked the mail that morning. There was a single 50-pound box.

Inside were birthday decorations, my favorite carrot cake mix and icing, a homemade CD he'd burned for me, and more than a dozen packets of instant Thai noodles from the restaurant where we'd had our first date. And tucked in the corner was a plastic Mr. T keychain that shouted, "I pity the fool!" when you squeezed it, an inside joke between us.

The box should have felt like love. And in some ways, it did. I smiled. I cried. But the tears didn't feel clean; they stung.

Because the last time a birthday box made me feel genuinely seen, I had been eight years old. That kind, old gentleman from the food bank had left it on our doorstep: cake, gifts, crayons, tenderness directed at the real me, not a polished version. He knew I grew up poor, without a dad consistently in my life, without food, without a lot, and he still showed compassion and generosity.

Timothy saw the version I'd created for him. He loved the woman who looked put-together, competent, and strong, the woman who always said the right thing and kept the darker parts of her story hidden. I never showed him the girl who had grown up hungry for safety, for protection, for belonging. I kept her locked away. So, his thoughtful gift didn't reach her. It couldn't. The wall was too high.

I told him thank you. I meant it. But underneath, all I felt was the gap between who I really was and who he believed he was loving. I wanted to deserve that box. I didn't.

And while I was deployed, I slipped into the only pattern I knew: running, hiding, reaching for someone that kept me from facing myself. I betrayed him. Recklessly. I numbed with attention and the illusion of being wanted. And every lie I told widened the space between us.

When the deployment was over and my plane finally landed in Baltimore, Timothy was waiting at the gate with balloons, champagne, our friends, and a limo idling outside. He'd been planning that moment for months, imagining it as a reunion; I had been dreading it.

By then, I had been gone longer than we had been together. Whatever genuine connection I once had with him had disappeared, lost in the arms of someone else during those long, quiet months in the Middle East. I did my best to play the role. To be who he remembered. But that kind of illusion wasn't one I was good at. Not with him. Not anymore.

Our first night back at the apartment, he reached for me, eager, hopeful. He wanted closeness. Reconnection. Intimacy. Something that felt like home again. But something in me just couldn't. Or maybe I wouldn't. I didn't want him anymore. And it broke his heart. He didn't say it, but I saw it. I felt it in the way his hand lingered too long without mine meeting it. In the way he studied my face like he was searching for a sign that I was still there.

I tried to make myself feel something. Anything. But I couldn't. So, I told him the truth I thought he could handle, that a lot had happened over the past nine months and I needed some time to decompress. He tried to hide his disappointment, but I could feel the ache in his silence.

The confusion he didn't voice. The kind of pain that makes you question if love was ever real or just something you imagined into being.

Late that night, he gently woke me. "Your phone keeps ringing," he said softly. "It might be something important."

It was just after three a.m. All I wanted was sleep, but I picked it up. On the other end was my mother's longtime friend, Sadiye. Her voice trembled. She told me the hospital had tried several times to send a Red Cross message while I was redeploying, but it must have gotten lost.

"Your mother had a massive heart attack," she said. "She's in surgery now, triple bypass. The doctors aren't sure she's going to make it."

My breath caught in my throat. But then her voice changed. Slower. Heavier. "There's something else I need to tell you," Sadiye said. "Something you deserve to know. Something I can't let die with her." I froze.

And then she said it, the truth that shattered whatever was left of the foundation I had been clinging to. "David … isn't your real father."

If I hadn't already been sitting upright in bed, I think I would've collapsed. Timothy was beside me, listening in stunned silence. He grabbed my hand. Grounded me.

Sadiye continued, "Your mother had an affair. His name is Hardy Crumby. He's your biological father." She apologized for telling me this way, over the phone, in the middle of the night, but she said I had a right to know. She urged me to fly to Seattle. To be with my mother. To make peace, if I could. And she promised to share whatever she remembered when I arrived.

The weight of war was still pressing against my shoulders. My relationship was unraveling. And now, the very core of my identity had been pulled out from under me. I wept. Not politely. Not quietly. But deeply. Painfully. The kind of weeping that comes from the hollow place underneath language, where grief and truth collide.

Timothy tried to hold me. Tried to comfort me. But I didn't want comfort. I didn't want touch. In that moment, the tattered tapestry of my life unraveled right in front of me. But as always before, I folded it up inside me and stuffed it away. The grief. The confusion. The fury. The shame. I repacked my suitcase and boarded the next flight to Seattle.

My mother survived the surgery, and I was there when she woke up. She was surprised. Grateful to be alive and grateful her daughter stood there beside her. Our relationship had always been strained, shallow at best. Now it was layered with silence, confusion, and questions too big to ask. As selfish as I'd been in so many areas of my life, I knew this wasn't the moment for confrontation. Not while she lay there, her chest stitched together, her heart literally learning to beat again. So, I did what I had learned to do best. I tucked the truth away, into that familiar, quiet space inside me where I could retrieve it later when I was ready. When I was stronger.

There was no anger. No confrontation. Just a simple truth. She was my mother, and I was glad she was alive. I stayed in Seattle for just over a week, partly to make sure my mother had the care and support she needed. And partly to give myself some space from Timothy: time to breathe, to think, to figure out what I wanted. It was all too much to deal with at once. So, like always, I dealt with the parts I could and set the rest aside.

When I returned to Maryland, I carried with me a quiet, cautious hope. A strained sort of optimism. Maybe we could still find our way back to each other. Maybe there was something left to salvage. Over the next couple of years, we developed a rhythm. It wasn't romance; it was more like a friendship. Roommates. But it was enough to keep me there. There was no passion. No real intimacy. Just a quiet, well-mannered roommate dynamic that neither of us had the courage to question. He had his routines; I had mine. He spent time with his friends; I spent time with mine. We hosted poker and game nights, cooked dinner, paid bills, and argued about my spending.

It wasn't love. It was logistics. Predictable. Functional. And for someone raised on chaos, that kind of stillness felt unsafe. I didn't know how to live in the absence of drama. Boredom made me restless. Routine made me reckless.

And yet, Timothy became my stability in a world that had never stopped spinning. He was steady, so steady it unnerved me. The safety he offered should have felt like peace, but instead, it exposed the parts of me that didn't know how to rest. I had been conditioned to brace for impact, to flinch at calm because calm never lasted. So even as I longed for his consistency, I kept waiting for it to turn into something else, something familiar. Something loud. Something broken.

We had talked about getting married and planned a grand wedding at the Maryvale Castle. A real-life fairy tale. But before the big day arrived, I received orders to change duty stations from Maryland to South Korea. So instead, we had a quiet ceremony at one of our favorite hiking spots in Patapsco State Park. A few close friends. Our two red Dobermans, which I snuck in against park rules. It was sweet. Familiar. But not special. Not the kind of sacred celebration you hope for with your only wedding. It felt rushed. Tense. Off-kilter for reasons we both felt but never named. Just weeks later, I was in another country. Again. And that's when everything began to change.

While I was in Korea, I was recruited to become part of the Army's most elite force: 1st Special Forces Operational Detachment Delta. Delta Force is a highly secretive special operations unit focused on counterter-rorism, hostage rescue, and direct-action missions. By then, I had already taken part in and even led high-level national security investigations and operations. And when locked in, I was good. Really good.

I built trust with foreign nationals in senior decision-making roles; one even called me his "Turkish Daughter." I elicited intelligence that directly satisfied national-level collection priorities. Urban surveillance may not have been for me. But source operations? Vulnerability analysis? Gain-ing access to high-trust environments even as a woman in conservative Middle Eastern spaces? That's where I thrived. I had a gift. I could read a room. Navigate cultural barriers with quiet precision. Slip into spaces where no one expected me and earn the respect of people who had no reason to give it.

As part of the Delta Force selection process, I was chosen to attend a highly specialized training, Strategic Debriefing, an advanced interroga-tion and operational support training and certification. I did well in that course. And people noticed.

One of them was a tall, striking Navy officer who looked like he could've replaced Richard Gere in *An Officer and a Gentleman*, Lt. Tebbe.

We were paired together a few times. We started spending time outside of training: hiking, talking, getting to know each other. Tebbe treated me with a gentleness I wasn't used to. On one hike, word came down that dangerous, undocumented individuals had been spotted in the area. He didn't flinch. He took charge. Kept me close. Protected. Safe. For the first time in my life, I felt safe in the presence of a man.

Tebbe was married. And so was I. But somewhere between professionalism and vulnerability, something shifted. My good friend Sarah, from my Advanced training days, was stationed in Arizona at the time and invited me out for my birthday. I also invited Tebbe, and he met me there. We drank. We danced. And later, he walked me to my room. That night, I lost myself in the comfort of his arms.

Somehow, in that moment, I convinced myself that he was the one. That he was my way out of the marriage I had built on fear: fear of being alone, fear of starting over, fear that no one would ever truly love me if they knew who I really was. I wanted to be with Tebbe. And he wanted to be with me. He hadn't fallen for a fabrication. I hadn't had time to build one. He saw me. And he still said he loved me. So, it had to be real. Right?

Like my mother, I fell in love with a man outside my marriage. And like her, I began an affair built on the hopeful promise that we would leave our spouses so we could be together. Another lie. One I told him. And myself. Because I wasn't going to leave Timothy. No matter how unloved I felt, I didn't have the courage. I was a coward. And the guilt I carried told me I didn't deserve happiness anyway. What I never stopped to consider was what Timothy deserved. Even as I wallowed in my shame, I never acknowledged the truth: He deserved far more than I could ever give.

Tebbe and I stayed in touch after returning to our duty stations: he in Virginia, me finishing my tour in Korea. We talked every day. About a future. A life together. Plans built on fantasy.

Eventually, I flew back to Maryland to spend time with Timothy. He had planned a weekend in New York with fancy dinners, Broadway shows, and a chance to reconnect. But the night before we left, I got sick. I couldn't stop going to the bathroom. Classic UTI symptoms. I asked him to take me to urgent care. Blood and urine tests. Long wait.

Finally, the nurse walked in. "So, what brings you in today?"

Half-laughing, I joked, "Probably pregnant. And have a UTI."

She smiled. "Well, you're right. You're both."

We froze. And the first words out of my mouth, words Timothy would never forget, were, "Oh no."

He looked at me, confused. But I knew. Deep in my bones. He wasn't the father. In that instant, everything changed. Delta Force was off the table. Pregnancy meant disqualification. I was devastated. I didn't want a baby; I didn't want anything that would tether me to the ground.

But when I looked at Timothy again, tears filled his eyes. His smile was pure. Joyful. He lifted me up, whispering, "I'm going to be a dad."

I stared at him, at the wonder in his eyes, the kind of wonder I had always dreamed someone might have for me. But instead of feeling cherished, I felt sick. Like an imposter watching someone else's fairy tale unfold, knowing I didn't belong in it. In that moment, I decided I would give him the fairy tale. I would become the wife he believed in. We would raise this baby. Start a family. He deserved that. Whether I wanted it or not. And like a cruel echo of my mother's life, another life was conceived in the shadows of secrecy. And that shadow would follow me long after the sun came up.

CHAPTER 9

Running Doesn't Work Anymore

I THOUGHT I could outrun it all: my guilt, the lies, the consequences. But when I called Tebbe, I knew the running was over. I told him we needed to meet. Immediately. I had to tell him face to face that I was pregnant and that I was certain the baby was his. To my surprise, he wasn't angry. He wasn't even confused. He was hesitantly happy. But I think he could hear the fear, the absence of joy in my voice. When he tried to hold me, I pulled away.

Still, he leaned in, trying to build a future around what I had just told him. He talked about Germany. He had already told his wife he wanted a divorce. His orders had come through, and he would be relocating. This, to him, was the perfect opportunity. A clean slate. A fresh start. A family. He told me I could leave the Army, and that he would support me fully. I could stay home and raise our baby or pursue whatever dream I wanted. He just wanted me.

It was everything I thought I had wanted. A life so different from the chaos I had always known. But deep down, I didn't believe I deserved it. I couldn't accept that kind of love. That kind of redemption. So, I told him a lie, a lie I convinced myself was a kindness. I told him I didn't love him. That what we had was only physical. That I had decided to raise the baby with Timothy.

I'll never forget the look on his face—confusion carved into heartbreak. He had walked away from everything for me. And I couldn't even meet him halfway. I was too afraid. Too afraid of the unknown. Too afraid of the consequences of truth, because, for most of my life, the truth had never served me. So, I let him go. I set him free to find the life his heart was searching for. And I carried the regret, the what-ifs. What if I had just followed my heart? What if I had chosen truth instead of fear? But I didn't. Instead, I returned to the prison I had built for myself. For the first year, I told myself it didn't matter. That my husband didn't know. That no one did. But the truth unravels itself.

Right before Austin was born, I left active duty but stayed in the intelligence community as a government contractor. I had years of operational experience, a high-level clearance, and suddenly I was being offered a six-figure salary, more money than I ever imagined someone without a college degree could earn. But instead of celebrating with me, Timothy began to resent it. To him, I hadn't "earned" that salary the way he had. Not with a degree. Not with credentials. Not the "right" way.

He wasn't impressed by the work or the sacrifices that had gotten me there. He was unsettled by what it meant. I was now the breadwinner. And money mattered to him. A lot.

Looking back, I know now that I was smart. I excelled academically. But I lived in a constant state of survival for so long that I never learned how to think about the future, college, career, or trajectory. My only goal was to get through each day safely. Timothy grew up differently. He had support. He had options. He had a net under him that I never had.

After five years of active duty, he left the Army and easily transitioned into a civilian government role, doing almost exactly what he'd done in Det 13. The pay increase wasn't dramatic, but the title, the prestige, the sense of importance, that mattered to him. Sometimes more than the work itself.

He was going to be TDY for a couple of months. His old Mustang, a beat-up yard ornament by then, sat in the backyard, wasting away at the same rate as our relationship. He had recently bought a new car, a Dodge Charger with the HEMI. Four doors, sure, but still a muscle car. It still had that growl. We used to love cars; that had once been our thing.

So, with my new salary and a generous sign-on bonus, I wanted to surprise him. To do something kind. Something connective. I had the Mustang towed and restored. New soft top. New tires. Suspension, clutch, paint correction. Full detailing. She was better than new. And I was so excited for him to see it.

I picked him up from the airport in it, buzzing with anticipation. We walked out to the parking lot. I watched his eyes move across the sleek black paint, the new soft top, the subtle hum of restoration I had labored to orchestrate behind the scenes. I had brought it back to life for him because I thought maybe, just maybe, bringing something old and broken back to life would breathe something back into us, too.

He simply shook his head. "Well, that was a waste of money. At least I can sell it now."

And less than a week later, that is exactly what he did. He sold it. I stood there, quietly stunned, trying to pretend I wasn't hurt. But the truth was that car had become a symbol. Of something that once meant everything. Something weathered but still worth restoring. And his indifference wasn't just about a car. It mirrored the ache I had carried for so long. That when people get too close, they find out you're not what they imagined. That when things get hard or messy or complicated, they leave.

It touched that deep, familiar place in me where fear whispered, *You are replaceable. You are forgettable.* It reminded me of how quickly things, and people, can be discarded when they no longer serve a purpose. And if I am being honest, maybe I wasn't just trying to fix a car. Maybe I was trying to prove that something broken could still be worth keeping. Maybe I was trying to prove I could be worth keeping. But he let the Mustang go, and a part of me went with it.

Nine months of pregnancy passed in a blur, and when they placed baby Austin in my arms, everything else in the world went quiet. Something broke through the thick, guarded walls I had spent years building around my heart. Something innocent. Something real.

Love: unselfish, unconditional, unshakeable.

I was overwhelmed, flooded by a kind of love I had never felt, never received, never known how to give. All I wanted was to protect him, to shield him from the pain and ugliness I had lived through, to give him the kind of life I once begged God for.

I couldn't see it clearly then, but looking back, I recognize what that moment was, a glimpse of a love I had only ever heard described in a little Pentecostal church in Belton, Texas. For the first time in my life, I touched the edge of God's heart. I remember thinking, *How could someone as wounded as me be trusted with something so pure? So beautiful? So innocent?*

But Austin gave me a reason. Not to pretend, but to change. He became the first person I ever wanted to be better for. And I was determined to give him the kind of love I never got.

For a while, I tried to make life with Timothy feel stable. We had a rhythm. It wasn't love, but it was order. Then, a few months into that new reality, he volunteered for a strategic deployment in Europe. He left me, still a brand-new mother, to figure things out on my own.

With Timothy deployed, I was presented with an opportunity, one that felt like both an escape and a step forward. Through my work, I was offered the chance to lead a team in Hawaii under Special Operations Command Pacific (SOCPAC). For a full year, Austin and I would live on the island while Timothy remained in Europe.

My job was to help develop more efficient processes for analyzing raw intelligence reports, coordinating those findings to support planning and operations across the Pacific theater. From deterring aggression, to responding to crises, to defeating threats to United States' interests, I found myself contributing to real-world missions with global reach.

And somehow, in the middle of that responsibility, I was also learning how to be a mother. I began to realize I was strong and capable of doing this on my own. Quietly, I started planning my exit from the marriage.

Christmas was especially important to Timothy, not just because it was Christmas but because it was also his birthday. That year, Timothy reached out and asked if I would meet him in California with Austin to spend Christmas with his family. I agreed, thinking maybe this would be the moment I would finally tell him the truth. Maybe this would be the clean break, the reset. Maybe I could finally start over, with just Austin and me.

By then, Timothy's family had grown more tender toward me or at least more cordial to my face. I would later see text messages that made his family's true feelings painfully clear, especially from his mother. But she was kind to me in person, and everyone adored Austin. That part wasn't fake.

So, like I had done many times before, and like I would do again, I swallowed the pain of how I was treated to make space for the love and kindness my sweet, innocent baby deserved. I would take a million bullets for that child. He was my world and the only thing that mattered. But when the moment came, I didn't tell the truth. Maybe it was the comfort of familiarity. Maybe it was the warmth of the holiday. Maybe I was still just a coward. Whatever it was, I let the silence stretch further. I watched Timothy board his flight back to Europe, and I returned to Hawaii with Austin.

And a couple of months later, I learned I was pregnant again, expecting our second child. Another tether. Another thread tying me to a life that had long passed its expiration date. But I clung to the one thing that still brought me joy, motherhood. I threw myself into work and into loving my son with everything I had. And for a while, that was enough.

Shortly before Jacob was born, my time in Hawaii came to an end, and I moved back to Maryland with Timothy. Things were not good. The pregnancy was difficult: physically, emotionally, and spiritually. Whatever was left of the connection between us had begun to unravel completely. We didn't like each other anymore. We argued constantly. The stress of it all wore me down to the bone, and as the cracks widened between us, Timothy's quiet suspicion began to grow. He waited. Watched. And then he acted.

A secret DNA test confirmed what his heart already knew about Austin.

I came home from work one day, and he was waiting. Calm. Too calm. He grabbed a piece of mail off the desk and handed it to me. "Can you explain this?" he asked. I looked down and saw it: the lab results. Everything in me froze. The part of me that knew how to lie, how to redirect, how to deny, shut down. There was no spinning this. No story to cover it. Only silence. And then, empty apologies.

He hurled questions at me, rage and betrayal crackling in every word, and all I could do was stand there, hollow, answering what I could and dodging what I couldn't. Then he looked at me, his eyes dark, his voice trembling and said what would haunt me forever. "You're just like your mother." And he was right. The heavy truth I had spent every second of every day trying to conceal was out, whether I was ready or not.

We tried for a day or two to hold the pieces together. We told ourselves we needed time. Space. But the damage had already been done. The fracture became a fault line. Resentment calcified into something immovable, just as it had for my father, David. And yet, like David, no, better than David, Timothy looked at me, eyes filled with tears and burning with grief, and said, "I don't care who you slept with; that boy is my son."

And I believed him. I knew no matter what I had done, no matter how much I had shattered us, he would love and protect both boys with everything he had. The love he once had for me was gone. But the love he had for them? Unshakable.

And in that moment, I saw another glimpse of God's mercy, not for me but for the two innocent children who didn't deserve to suffer because of my mistakes. Once again, like my mother, I found myself trapped in the cycle. Love turned to pain. Pain turned to survival. I thought I was different. I thought I was free. But I was just another echo.

Things started to turn violent between us. Neither of us wanted to raise children in that kind of environment. So, I took the boys and moved closer to my work in Quantico, Virginia. Timothy stayed behind in Maryland. I hired a kind, nurturing *au pair* from Brazil to help care for my boys so I could keep working. Timothy moved into an apartment and began taking the boys for a few hours at a time on the weekends. I was still nursing our youngest, so they didn't stay overnight yet.

It was a hard, confusing time. On one hand, I could finally breathe. The truth was out. No more pretending. No more hiding. But I was also drowning in shame. In guilt. In the sharp, ever-present sting of failure. I wasn't just living with the consequences of my choices; I was living in the shadow of every choice my mother ever made.

CHAPTER 10

Planted in Darkness

I WAS SHRINKING in Virginia, under the pressure of maintaining my performance at work, under the weight of trying to be the kind of mother my sons deserved, under the suffocating need to be better than what I had growing up. And I could no longer manage that alone. Meanwhile, Timothy had volunteered for another deployment overseas, and I knew I couldn't do it by myself anymore. So, I told him: I want to move back home. Back to Texas. Closer to family.

I had been in touch with my old youth pastors, Ricky and Annette. When they heard I was considering coming back, they immediately offered support for the boys and for me. The kind of emotional and spiritual covering I never received from my parents, David and Norma. Texas still didn't feel completely like home, but it was the closest thing I had. I wanted to raise my sons in a place that moved slower than the East Coast. A place with charm and quiet. A small town where they could be little boys for a while longer, where life didn't always feel like a race. But it was more than that.

Something deeper was stirring inside me. A quiet pull I couldn't explain, a tug on my heart that felt like a longing for something real. Something steady. Something constant. I didn't understand it at the time, but now I know it was God. And even though I couldn't name it then, Annette could. She had always been more than a youth pastor to me; she was a spiritual mother. A woman who carried both gentleness and strength in equal measure. I felt safe with her. Understood.

She had seen something in me when I was a teenager, beneath the attitude, beyond the hardened exterior I used to protect myself. And I admired her deeply. Not just for her grace and compassion, but for her faith. Annette had endured a storm greater than I could fathom, one I feared I would never survive. She lost her daughter in a tragic car accident. The kind of loss that should have shattered her completely, but it didn't. She kept trusting God. She kept serving others. She kept loving. To me, that was real strength. The kind I had only ever pretended to have.

Timothy agreed that moving back to Texas was best for the boys and me. We sold the luxury SUV that I could no longer afford, as six-figure jobs weren't exactly lining the streets in Belton, especially not for someone without a degree. And there weren't any foreign nationals to track or classified operations to run; that life was behind me. I left behind the finery of my proverbial Egypt, with two young sons in tow, and headed toward the unknown, hoping to find my own promised land. No job. No home. A little money. And faith in something I didn't yet understand.

We moved into one of Ricky and Annette's spare bedrooms. By then, they were pastors of their own church and ran a daycare, which they graciously let the boys attend for free while I looked for work. It helped more than they knew. But when some members of their congregation found out, anger followed quickly. They confronted Ricky and Annette, insisting it was unfair that my children were allowed to attend for free when theirs weren't. They wanted to know why I deserved "special treatment."

And just like that, the support ended.

Within a couple of weeks, I had already become an inconvenience. I went to church with Ricky and Annette, but it was impossible to feel at home in a congregation that looked at me with resentment simmering behind their eyes. The attention was uncomfortable, painfully familiar.

Still, I'll always be grateful for Ricky and Annette. They opened their home to me, offered love, and helped me find a job as a secretary at the local VA hospital. It was exactly the help I needed in that season.

I eventually found a house to rent, slightly outside my means, but in the best school zone in Belton. It was nice enough that I didn't look like a failure from the outside, and that mattered more than I wanted to admit.

Coming back to my hometown was harder than I expected, as no one understood the world I had come from or the work I had done. I had been part of something few people would ever comprehend, and suddenly, that life was gone. My pride went with it. Looking back now, I can see it was by design.

I went from serving as director of counterintelligence analytic operations at a top defense contracting firm, with the highest-level clearance, to fetching coffee for a supervisor who walked past the coffee room just to tell me to bring her a cup. It was humbling. And I didn't last long.

After watching my supervisor parade me around the office and introduce me to other supervisors as her "special agent secretary," something in me snapped. I told her exactly where she could shove her extra-hot, French vanilla, no sugar cup of coffee, and I quit. One reality check after another stripped me down.

I started selling off the luxuries I'd collected over the years: designer bags, shoes, custom furniture, and textiles. All the expensive armor I had used to disguise my brokenness. I got top dollar for most of it, but it didn't feel like winning. It felt like being exposed, because now I had no job. And I had children to care for. I needed to go back to school. Somehow. But I had no direction. No idea what I wanted to do next. I only knew one thing: I was broken, in every sense of the word. And whatever good was left in me, whatever was still salvageable, would have to come from God. For the sake of my children.

I applied and was accepted into the Christian Studies program at the University of Mary Hardin–Baylor (UMHB). I wanted to know God, more than anything. I wanted to know who He was. Why He allows the pain and hurt He does. I wanted to know who I was and what my purpose was in His plan. Thanks to my veterans' benefits, I only had to work part-time. The monthly stipend I received was not much, but it was just enough to help us scrape by. There were a million other majors I could have pursued, programs that would have led to more obvious careers, more stability, but I followed God's call, not knowing where it would lead me.

I carried a deep thirst for truth, a desire to go further than what Sunday sermons and personal Bible reading had ever taken me. But as I studied the Bible, I struggled to connect with it. It felt angry at times, harsh in others. Cold. Cryptic. I couldn't reconcile the God I had encountered in glimpses, with my babies in my arms, with grace showing up in small, unexpected ways, with the God I saw on the page.

I wondered if maybe what I needed was a deeper understanding: academic, historical, philosophical. Maybe if I could learn the Bible in its original contexts, its languages, its landscapes, something would unlock. Maybe then the stories that felt tangled and confusing would finally make sense.

UMHB was a Baptist college. I had grown up in a non-denominational, borderline Pentecostal church and, at the time, was attending Ricky and Annette's hybrid version of both. The teachings were different; not contradictory but in my church, things were taken more literally. And the more I learned in my classes, the more questions I had. I did what I thought was right. I went to Ricky, my pastor, with my questions. I came with a genuine heart and was not looking to undermine or challenge; I was looking to understand. But he did not like my questions. To this day, I am not sure if it was the way I asked or the questions themselves, but I will never forget what he said: If I kept going down the road I was on at that Baptist school, he did not see a place for me in his ministry.

I was stunned. How could a hunger to understand God more deeply, through study, history, and language, disqualify me from ministry? The rejection burned. And for years, it stayed with me. I left their church and stopped speaking to Ricky and Annette. For more than a decade, there was silence between us.

It was a painful season. They had been my family when I had none. I wanted to make them proud, but I also wanted to honor God. I wanted to "get it right." And in my heart, I believed that seeking deeper understanding was part of obedience, not rebellion. But even in that heartbreak, one truth remains: Ricky and Annette were the ones who lifted me when I had nothing left. They pointed me to God when I was at rock bottom.

They planted a seed of faith and hunger I couldn't yet name. And like many things formed in the unseen, its roots grew strongest in the dark.

A Chinese bamboo seed doesn't break the surface for years, remaining buried in the dark, invisible to the eye, and people assume it's not growing. But underground, it draws nutrients from the soil and absorbs the living water. Its roots stretch wide and deep, forming a strong network of rhizomes that store energy and prepare for what's coming. And then, when the time is right, it bursts through the surface.

Once it breaks through, bamboo grows fast. Wild. Towering. Some species can shoot up feet in just days. It's unrelenting. Resilient. Some suggest it's invasive. A nuisance. But I say it's unstoppable. And I think God knew that's what He was doing with me.

Like Timothy did before when Austin was born, he volunteered again for an overseas assignment. I believe now this is how he coped when the world felt too heavy: he hid and buried himself in work and saved money. That has always been a security for him. We Skyped when he was able, mostly so he could see and talk to the boys. He would send money from time to time, but it was inconsistent. There was no real financial support, as he kept his money separate from us. Still, when we spoke, he asked about how the boys liked Texas. About the home we were starting. About my classes. There was a kind curiosity in his voice that felt genuine, and I appreciated that. But even in the kindness, there was an undercurrent, a low simmer of blame and resentment that never fully went away. We had never filed any paperwork to legally dissolve our marriage, but Timothy made it clear, without question, that we were over.

During that time, I began an internship with a local pastor, author, and speaker I'd first heard during one of our college's mandatory chapel services. Sean Palmer talked about Jesus, and about life, in a way that resonated deeply with me. His message carried none of the dogma, performance, or religious trappings I had grown so weary of. He spoke with honesty and clarity, telling the truth in a way that felt like it came from the heart of Jesus Himself.

When he finished speaking and began gathering his things, I rushed to the stage. I introduced myself, shared a bit of my background, and asked if his church offered any internship opportunities. His church was non-denominational but rooted in the principles of the Church of Christ. The denominational differences didn't matter to me. I wasn't looking for perfect theological alignment; I was looking for truth. For mentorship. For someone who knew how to hold both story and Scripture with reverence and depth.

Sean became far more than a brilliant speaker or gifted writer; he became one of my dearest friends. A safe, trustworthy adult male in my life who never asked for anything in return. He offered wisdom, guidance, encouragement, and opportunities, with no strings attached. He saw me. Not the mask. Not the polished strength. But the mess underneath. And somehow, I felt safe enough to let him see. I think he understood how heavy that was for me, how much it cost to be seen without armor. He honored it and held it with grace.

Sean was also the first person who encouraged me to write, long before I believed I could. I hope he reads this one day and understands the depth of his impact on my life. I don't know if I'll ever be half the writer or speaker he is, but I hope this memoir makes him proud. I hope he sees, as he did then, that something strong, something true, did grow from the darkness I was buried in.

CHAPTER 11

The Curtain Call

RECENTLY, MY TWO oldest boys told me they overheard their dad talking with someone about one of his biggest regrets: volunteering for deployments after they were born. For a moment, I felt a flicker of validation. During that season, I was struggling to make ends meet, slipping back into survival mode again, sacrificing what I could, stretching every dollar, doing whatever it took to keep us afloat. Even if Timothy never said it to me, part of me wanted to believe that Timothy finally recognized how careless and selfish it was to leave me alone to figure everything out.

But then my son Jacob continued, "Not because it was hard for you raising us by yourself, but because he thinks we would've turned out better if he was more involved."

There it was, that familiar condescending, narcissistic tone, now coming from my son's mouth instead of his. I felt my defenses rise instantly, the urge to argue with words spoken in a room I wasn't in. But I swallowed it. Austin and Jacob were only repeating what they'd heard; I refused to drag them into the emotional tug-of-war I would spend years being baited into. Still, I could see the words unsettled them, and they unsettled me.

But I wasn't ready to unpack it with them, not while my anger and grief still sat so close to the surface.

And hearing Timothy twist their story struck a nerve, not because it was true but because I remembered exactly what it took to survive those years. My sons didn't turn out great in spite of his absence. They turned out great because they are strong, compassionate, intelligent young men, because I showed up every single day, and because God was present through it all.

Even when their father chose himself, God never left us. While those baby boys were still in my womb, God was already crafting purpose, planting calling, writing the story of who they would become. Their lives were never dependent on the presence or absence of another person. They were held. Covered. Designed with intention.

Some seasons felt impossible. And somehow, by the grace of God, things always worked out. But there is one moment I will never forget, Jacob's first birthday. We were living paycheck to paycheck and stretching every dollar until it snapped. His birthday weekend fell on a long weekend, and I wouldn't be paid until Saturday, the same day as his party. I had just enough money to buy some cupcakes, a few modest gifts, basic decorations, and a small bounce house rented at an incredibly generous and discounted rate from an old friend.

It was Jacob's first birthday, and I refused to let him feel the kind of disappointment I remembered from my own childhood. I didn't care what I had to sacrifice. My children would know celebration, even if I had to build it out of scraps.

But I also had a disconnect notice from the water company. I called and begged them to wait until Monday. They couldn't; my extensions had run out. On Wednesday afternoon, the water was shut off.

I picked the boys up from daycare and drove home, trying to figure out how I was going to make this work. But the moment we walked through the door, I felt it, the silence of a house missing something essential. A different kind of quiet. A quiet that pressed in.

"Mommy, the toilet won't flush! The water's broke!" Austin said, confused.

I gave him a simple excuse he could understand and glanced at the cases of bottled water in the pantry. Then I got an idea. "We're going to camp in the living room tonight," I told him. "We're gonna play Army, just like when Mommy was in Iraq."

I used water bottles to fill the toilet tank, to wash our hands, to make dinner and do the dishes. I showed them how Mommy had to brush her teeth in Iraq, how we made do with what we had. I poured water into their little hands so they could wash their faces and brush their teeth. I heated water on the stove so they could take a bath. All the while, I fought back tears. Tears laced with shame. With exhaustion. With the quiet ache of failure. I stayed strong long enough to pitch our four-man tent in the living room, roll out sleeping bags, pass out stuffed animals, and wait for them to fall asleep.

Then I slipped into the bathroom, shut the door, and cried. I cried in shame. In anger. In heartbreak. I was sure that moving back to Texas had been something God called me to do. So why would He bring me out of Egypt, part the Red Sea, only to let me die in the wilderness? It felt cruel. Like karma. And deep down, I believed I deserved it; that is what I told myself. That is what I told God, if He was even listening. "I deserve this," I whispered. "But they don't. My babies don't."

I cried until my legs went numb. Then I cleaned myself up and crawled into the tent, pulling them close. I watched their peaceful, sleeping faces, so innocent, so unaware of the storm we were in. And in that moment, God gave me peace. I was wearing stress like a second skin. But that night, I had done my job. I had protected their joy. Preserved their innocence. That night, I was a good mom.

The next morning, I woke up to a notification on my phone, two deposits had been made in my bank account. My monthly stipend came early because of the long weekend. And Timothy had sent money for Jacob's birthday. I paid the water bill immediately. Bought a few more presents, and by the time we arrived back home, the water was back on.

And, like a soft hug from Heaven, smiling, talking about how fun camping in the living room had been. "Can we do it again tonight, Mommy?" they asked. I smiled and said yes. This time, with the water running. Even in Iraq, even in the middle of a war, we eventually had running water. And if we could find it there, I had to believe God would bring it here too, in this quiet battlefield I was now fighting in.

Over the next several months, Timothy and I talked a lot. More than we ever had. He had questions. A thousand of them. He wanted the truth, the whole of it. And I owed him that. I told him everything. I took every insult. Every verbal punch. Every drop of pain he needed to release. Not because I had no defense, but because I believed I had to take it. For the boys' sake. So, I did. Timothy told me he still loved me. That he did not know if he could ever forgive me, but he wanted to try. I was a shell of myself. Hollowed. Broken. But I still believed in one thing: my boys deserved a whole family. Even if that meant sitting in silence, absorbing every aftershock of the earthquake I caused, I would. For them.

There was no real plan for healing. No counseling. No road map. Just a "see how things go" between us. When Timothy returned from Afghanistan, we made plans for him to spend a few days in Texas before we all flew to California for Christmas as a family. When he walked through the arrivals gate, the boys screamed with joy, rushing into his arms. In that moment, the joy in the room drowned out the pain. It filled every corner. Their daddy was home, and he loved them. And they knew it.

A few days later, we drove to Dallas and stayed overnight at a hotel near the airport to make the early flight a little easier on the boys. That night, after they fell asleep, I was about to read while Timothy got ready to shower. He left his phone next to my book on the nightstand, and it buzzed.

And there it was. A message lit up the screen, "Stephanie Miller: I really missed not getting to talk tonight. Can't wait to feel your body again soon!"

My heart sank. Part disbelief. Part confirmation. Part relief. "Who's Stephanie Miller?" I asked.

Timothy's reaction was sharp. Defensive. "Why are you going through my phone?" he shot back.

"I wasn't. It lit up while I reached for my book."

His face twisted with self-righteous anger. "None of your business," he said. "I'm not a cheater like you."

The sting of it hit hard, but I was furious. I had memorized the number and called it in front of him. She answered. And I told her exactly who I was. "I'm his wife," I said. "And if you care about your career, you'll never call or see Timothy again. Your fling is over." She started to say something, but I hung up.

Timothy glared at me, furious. I looked him in the eye. "If you care about yours, I'd heed the same warning." I grabbed a pillow and left the room, slipping into the other bed with my boys.

When we arrived at LAX, Timothy's mom and stepdad were waiting. The tension hit before a word was spoken, the whispered side conversations, the tight smiles, the silence in the car. Every glance felt loaded. I expected them to know something was wrong. I didn't expect the performance. The Scarlet Letter Tour, and that's what it felt like.

Timothy was the golden child: beloved, protected, the son who could do no wrong. They wanted to see him. And their grandsons. Not the woman who had betrayed him. The gentle scoldings disguised as compassion. The "We all make mistakes" comments. The brittle encouragement wrapped in judgment. It was exhausting.

And even though I had just discovered Timothy had betrayed me, too, I said nothing. I didn't tell his family. I didn't expose him. I swallowed it whole. I smiled. I cared for the boys. And I quietly counted the days until it was over.

By the time we returned to Texas, the mask had slipped completely. We held our breath through every conversation, balancing on the tightrope of unresolved betrayal and years of resentment. It didn't take much for everything to break.

A hurricane poured out of me. We fought. We screamed. We hurled accusations like weapons. He threw a bottle of hot sauce; it hit me in the face. I slapped him. And then everything crossed a line.

I ran into our bedroom and slammed the door behind me. He followed me in and pinned me to the bed, pressing a pillow over my mouth and nose. I couldn't breathe. His eyes were vacant, cold, unfamiliar. I struggled beneath his weight, gasping, clawing for air, my vision tunneling. A wave of dizziness rolled over me, and for a terrifying second, I believed I was going to die. And then, suddenly, he stopped.

He jumped back as if waking from a trance, turned away, and sat silently, staring at the wall. The room felt cavernous. I lay there, stunned, gulping air, frozen in place. He began to cry. Then he crawled toward me on his knees.

"I'm sorry," he kept repeating. "I don't know what came over me."

But even in his apology, something was clear: He wasn't grieving what he'd done to me. He was grieving the loss of control. The shame of being caught in the ugliness he had always kept hidden from himself. And beneath his tears, I felt that he believed I deserved it. All of it.

I sat there, still catching my breath, still tasting fear on my tongue. And all I could do was look at him and whisper, "Just get away from me. I can't live like this anymore." It was the quietest sentence I had ever spoken, but somehow the truest.

In the days that followed, I began to piece myself back together. Not for Timothy. Not even for me. But for the boys. They deserved to see strength that wasn't angry. Resilience that wasn't silent suffering. Love that didn't wound or disappear.

There comes a moment when you don't just make a boundary; you *consecrate* one. A line in the sand that says: This stops with me. This will not pass to my children. Not one inch further.

Standing in the aftermath of that night, with the echo of violence still hanging in the air, I understood that this wasn't only about my survival; it was about theirs. About the kind of men my boys would become. About the kind of women they would one day love. I wasn't just leaving a marriage; I was ending a generational script. What they learned about love would come from the courage I showed right here, in the breaking.

But life doesn't wait for clean endings or tidy transitions. My divorce from Timothy was long, expensive, and emotionally brutal. There were moments I second-guessed myself, moments when the unknown future felt more terrifying than the familiar pain. I debated in my mind the same question Israel wrestled with in Exodus 14: *Was the bondage in Egypt better than the uncertainty of the wilderness?* At least bondage was predictable. At least I understood its rules.

It took me years to see the pattern clearly. I didn't know how to sit in discomfort; I didn't know how to walk through fire. I only knew how to find a shortcut, another relationship, another distraction, another way to bypass the process that was meant to develop something undeniable in me. Pain had trained me to leap from one burning building to another instead of learning how to rebuild my own foundation. I never stayed long enough in the wreckage to heal. I never let myself find a safe place to land and rest.

My divorce wasn't even final when I started dating Jeff. He was one of the T-ball dads who noticed me at practice: two boys close in age to mine, recently divorced, carrying wounds that were still open and raw. He made me laugh until my stomach hurt, made me feel beautiful at a time when I couldn't find my own worth in the mirror. But the truth is we were two broken hearts trying to drown our pain in companionship. It wasn't love; it was life support.

And yet, out of that imperfect beginning grew something unexpected, a friendship and a co-parenting relationship that, against every odd and stereotype, would become one of the healthiest I have ever heard of.

I found out I was pregnant a week before finishing my undergraduate degree, before my divorce was final, and right after being awarded the T.B. Maston Scholar award from my university. I felt like a walking contradiction in my own eyes, carrying honor in one hand and shame in the other. I wanted to disappear. To hide. To bury myself under anything that would silence the whispers I imagined everywhere around me. And in a small town like Belton, for a little while, the whispers were real.

Jeff was already moving on with someone else; it read like a tabloid headline. And for a moment, it felt like one too. But we had both survived too many storms, carried too many scars to let gossip write the story of this child's life. And if there was one thing no one could deny about me, it was this: I was a good mother. I would sacrifice anything for my children. And even in his brokenness, Jeff saw that in me. He respected it.

Then Alex arrived, a beautiful, healthy baby boy full of light, laughter, and wonder. His world may be far from traditional, but it is rich with love. He has a big, blended family of people who cherish him. And really, what more could a child ask for?

At thirty-three, I was a youth minister. Studying Christian theology. Preparing for seminary. And quietly carrying the weight of my own hypocrisy. A single mother of three boys. A heart full of contradictions. I did what I had to do to survive. I lied. I manipulated. I burned bridges just to keep my head above water. I told myself it was for my children. That my actions were justified. But the truth was I was running. Running from shame. Running from the truth. Running from the reflection of my mother in the choices I made.

Survival has a way of convincing you that coping is healing. It whispers that as long as you're functioning, you're fine. But I wasn't fine. I was hollow. Wearing masks to cover the shame. Rewriting reality in my mind just enough to keep moving forward. Spiritually exhausted. Emotionally fragmented. And deep down, I knew I couldn't keep running forever.

The most painful revelation wasn't just that I had become like my mother. It was that I finally understood her. I don't know everything my mother endured. I don't know what pain shaped her, what abuse or neglect filtered the way she saw herself, or the way she loved. I only know that she made choices that hurt me. And now I had made choices that hurt others. I don't believe she knowingly passed her brokenness down to me; she was trying to survive. Just like I was.

And the scar I carry today is likely the same one she hid under pride, silence, and strength. The beginning of change didn't come when I tried harder. It came when I finally looked at the scar I had inherited and decided to understand it instead of repeat it. Somewhere, the cycle had to stop. Someone had to stop it. Not with blame, but with grace. Not with denial, but with acknowledgment. I chose to be that someone. Not because I was stronger than my mother. But because I had been given the clarity to see the pattern, and the courage to break it.

CHAPTER 12

Quarter Turn to the Right

NOT EVERY TURN is graceful. Not every step forward feels like progress. After my youngest son was born, I found myself in another relationship that moved too fast, burned too hot, and unraveled even faster. On paper, it looked like love: in reality, survival, loneliness, and deception tangled into a tight knot. He was not a good man, though I didn't know it at first. We were married and divorced in less than six months. And that's all the space I'll give him here. He wasted enough of my time and doesn't deserve more of my words.

But if that chapter taught me anything, it was this: Loneliness can dress itself up as destiny. Desperation can look an awful lot like love when you're tired enough. And rushing what is meant to be slow, whether healing, trust, or growth, always costs more than you think it will. It was another scar. Another reminder that the work of rebuilding wasn't just physical. It was spiritual. Emotional. Invisible. And inevitable.

At that point, I was well beyond the threshold of failure, and I was tired of my own excuses. I was extremely depressed and struggling to show up emotionally for my children. I recognized it and knew something had to change. I asked for help. I started therapy and antidepressants. I got a gym membership. And I went to work on myself.

I started training at Gold's Gym in Copperas Cove. I had no idea what I was doing. I was athletic, but I wasn't the first pick for a team growing up. So, I did what I knew how to do. I researched. I printed a workout plan. And I showed up.

For a season, the gym became my church. And I've been part of several churches. Very few ever felt like a true community. But at the gym, I found something that strangely resembled fellowship more than many sanctuaries I'd sat in. And that's its own kind of indictment, when "love your neighbor" is a bumper sticker at church but lived out between strangers in a weight room.

It was a miracle I didn't break anything because I had no idea what I was doing at times. One evening, as I fumbled with the weights on an incline bench, a short but intimidating woman walked up to me. Angie didn't ask if I needed help; she already knew I needed it. She corrected my form, removed some of the weights, and invited me to join her shoulder workout.

"If you can't do it correctly at the lighter weight," she said, "you have no business struggling with the heavier weight."

She was right. And I was grateful. Later, I'd learn just how generous that moment was; working out with someone can be annoying. Most days, I preferred throwing on a hoodie, headphones on, and disappearing into the lift. But that night, I needed help, even if I wouldn't have asked for it. And Angie saw that. She stepped in anyway.

I didn't know it then, but God had sent me another blessing disguised as a gym buddy. If you haven't noticed a pattern by this point, look again. Throughout every trauma, every self-made disaster, every reckless decision, God kept slipping people into my life at the exact moment I needed them.

Angie became like a sister to me: no-nonsense, fiercely protective of her time, fiercely loyal to the people she loved. God didn't send a burning bush to lead me out of that season. He sent good people. Ordinary people. Strong people. People who showed up. And I consider myself incredibly blessed.

Through Angie, I met Rod from BeFit Gym in Killeen, another unexpected blessing at a time when I desperately needed one. Rod was funny, hardworking, and unafraid to call me out when I wasn't giving a hundred percent. He became a trusted coach and a friend. Rod taught me how to work hard. How to push past pain. How to be honest with myself. How not to accept the bare minimum. How to tap into a strength I didn't know I had.

He introduced me to the world of competitive bodybuilding and encouraged me to start training. The thought of stepping onto a stage in front of thousands, wearing a barely there Swarovski crystal–encrusted bikini and showcasing months of relentless discipline, sounded equal parts ridiculous and thrilling. What I didn't know then was just how hard I would have to work to earn that spot on stage. And there was no prancing. The posing alone was its own workout.

After several months of consistency, I found my rhythm. I found purpose. And I made serious gains. That year was a transformation: body, mind, and spirit. And I wasn't the only one sacrificing. My sons were sacrificing, too. The early mornings of cardio. The restrictive diets. The meal-prepping. The intense workouts and late recoveries. All while being Mom and teaching and coaching at a middle school. Some nights, after coming home late from work, picking them up, helping with homework, and squeezing in dinner, I would collapse from exhaustion.

We didn't always have money for Chick-fil-A, the unofficial "Mom's too tired to cook" meal. Some nights, I handed them my prepped meals instead. It wasn't glamorous. One evening when Jacob loudly protested and refused to eat fish and rice again, we laughed and went to Chick-fil-A. They deserved that much. A year of that grind, and I finally stepped onto the bodybuilding stage in a deep blue sparkly bikini, thirty-seven years old, and walked away with trophies in two categories. It was one of the biggest shows in Texas that year. And first-time competitors, especially women my age, rarely walk away with trophies. But I did. I worked my butt off, literally and figuratively.

Tasha, a new friend made in the gym and another working mom and competitor, brought my sons to the show. Their father was not in the habit of doing anything outside of his legally ordered obligations and sometimes not even that, but that's a story for another chapter. Tasha understood the sacrifice. She lived it, too. When it was time for the competitors to line up on stage, I heard my boys screaming behind the judges: "That's my mom!"

And when the commands came, "Face the rear," "Quarter turn to the left," "Quarter turn to the right," I shook like a cold wet dog at first. But seeing the pride on my boys' faces, hearing their voices, grounded me.

Somewhere between their pride and the music blasting through the speakers, something in me locked in. I slipped into the zone. I did exactly what I had practiced for almost a year. And when the judging was complete and the winners were announced, they called my name twice. I thanked God with my tears. I needed that win. My boys needed that win. Because while I had suffered, they had carried it too with resilient, innocent hearts. They never complained when we went without. They never resented me when Mommy needed thirty minutes behind a closed door just to breathe and cry. They never blamed me for the microwaved dinners. (Well, Jacob blamed me for the tilapia. Fair.)

They were my biggest cheerleaders. They watched their mom fall apart, kneel in prayer, and refuse to stay broken. They watched me rise. When I came off the stage holding my trophies, I scooped up the candy waiting backstage, filled the trophies with it, and ran to the boys. I handed the trophies straight to them. Because they weren't just mine. They were theirs too. They had cheered for me, sacrificed with me, and waited through late-night workouts and early-morning cardio. We earned those trophies together. We celebrated as a team, mother and sons.

Training for the stage taught me far more than how to build muscle. It taught me discipline at a level I had never known. It taught me consistency. Ownership. Sacrifice, the kind no one applauds. The kind that happens in silence, in small choices, in relentless decisions made when no one is watching.

It wasn't the crowd or the trophies that changed me. It was the quiet, daily decision to keep showing up. Even when it hurt. Even when I didn't believe in myself yet. Even when the world felt heavy. And somewhere in the repetition, in the sweat, the hunger, the discipline, something inside me learned how to stand again.

All the things I wanted and craved had to be put aside for later. The simple comforts. The indulgences. The moments of ease. It was incredibly challenging to deny those things day after day. But I did it. And in doing so, I proved something to myself. I proved I could do hard things, not just once but over and over again.

I remember the first bacon cheeseburger I had after the show. I took one bite and wept. It wasn't just a good burger that night; it was the best burger I had ever tasted. Because it wasn't seasoned with salt and pepper. It was seasoned with sacrifice.

Every bite reminded me of the journey, of everything I had laid down to get there, of what it cost me, of how much sweeter things taste when you wait for them. That's the thing about denial and discipline: When you wait, when you resist shortcuts, when you learn to sit in the discomfort, the reward is deeper. Richer. More meaningful.

God uses moments like that to bring revelation. I was so afraid of being stripped down and emptied of myself so God could rebuild me. Afraid to sit in the discomfort in other parts of my life. But I *could* do it.

Just like the weights and the nutrition changed my body, if I fully surrendered, the Lord wanted to change my heart. He was trying to get my attention, but I was still so angry and hurt, I couldn't see His heart.

The dangerous side of bodybuilding mirrored the dangerous side of pride: You can look incredibly strong while quietly tearing yourself apart. Because what looked like transformation on the outside, trophies, muscle, discipline, was actually a slow unraveling on the inside. I had pushed myself to the limit trying to reclaim control of my life, trying to outrun the grief, the fear, the exhaustion. But when my body broke, my spirit followed. And that's when I realized: I needed to rest.

After a severe back injury, I found myself in the ER, getting scans of my spinal cord. What they found wasn't just a herniated disc. They found cellular abnormalities, growths on my liver, ovaries, and cervix. Cancer. Surgery was a must. At the time, I had just started my Master of Arts in Counseling program. I tried to push through at first, but it cost me too much physically, mentally, and spiritually. I had to hit pause to take care of my health.

I walked away from my body much as I had walked away from relationships that betrayed me. I had nourished it, disciplined it, shaped it into something strong, and still, it broke. Cancer felt like the ultimate betrayal.

All that work, all that sacrifice, undone by something I couldn't control. I stopped trusting it. I stopped trusting myself. I pulled away from the very body I had fought to reclaim.

After treatments and surgeries, I slowly began to recover and return to my studies. A month into summer classes, my sister called me: my dad was dying. He stopped taking the medications he needed to take daily. He stopped eating. He wanted to die. This had been going on for weeks before my sister and I knew anything was happening, and it was only after our intervention that he was taken to the emergency room. The doctors explained that he was extremely malnourished and was experiencing organ failure; he was going to die, and they were just there to make him as comfortable as possible. He was suffering, and he was tired. And his death, while painful, ended that suffering.

The hard part about losing my dad was this: We were finally starting to have real conversations. We were finally talking about the future. I never got the chance to tell him that, despite all the things he did wrong, and all the things I did wrong, I was grateful for him. Grateful he tried to be a father to me when he didn't have to be. Grateful he pointed me toward Jesus, whom I would cling to when everything else fell apart. Grateful he took me to church. He planted seeds that took years to break through. But they grew. And for that, I honor him.

That year hit me in waves. The surgery, graduate school, my dad's death: it all came so close together. There was a month or two between each event, but it didn't feel like relief. It felt like being pulled under by the tide. Just when I'd muster the strength to reach the surface and gasp for air, another wave would come. And I'd go under again. Each time, I got a little more tired. A little more unsure if I'd make it back up. I didn't have time to process what I had lost or what I was still carrying. I just kept moving. Surviving. Trying not to drown.

I didn't realize how much the toll of that year had taken on me until late in the semester during Pre-Practicum. I just stopped showing up. Stopped doing the work. Stopped caring. There were so many responsibilities I was letting slip through my fingers. And before I knew it, I had stumbled into another dark hole. This time, I wasn't sure I knew the way out.

After years of trauma, survival, and stress, I was completely exhausted. My nervous system was completely overwhelmed. What my emotions managed to suppress, my body carried. There was so much in me, simmering just beneath the surface, waiting to erupt, and no dosage of antidepressants could numb it completely.

I didn't need another accomplishment. I didn't need another goal to chase. I needed rest. Real rest. Not the kind that feels like collapse, but the kind that comes when you finally lay your weapons down. When you stop fighting battles you were never meant to fight. The kind of rest that whispers, "You are still worthy, even when you are not producing."

I needed to walk away from the ladders I kept climbing to prove my value. It was time to stop performing. Time to stop pushing. Time to rest. Not as surrender, but as strength.

CHAPTER 13

The Apple Tree

SEVERAL YEARS ALMOST a decade earlier, when I learned the truth about my biological father, I waited several years before asking my mother questions. And only now do I truly understand just how painful that must have been for her, a truth she wasn't ready to tell, but one she could no longer hide or ignore. Using databases and resources I had access to at the time, I tried to track him down.

But I had limited information: A bronze/orange late '70s model Porsche 911. A vague location, somewhere in Texas, for about a year. Just enough details to give me a little hope. I managed to find his stepmother, Virgie, and his son, Sean. I sent his stepmother a letter and reached out to Sean via private message on Facebook.

His stepmother responded, but it led to a dead end. Sean responded too but was quick to say that after asking his dad, Hardy insisted he had no idea what I was talking about, that I was probably just some crazy person. Sean asked me not to contact him again. Not long after, I got a call from a blocked number. I almost didn't answer, but something told me to pick it up.

A man's voice, soft and hesitant, said, "Hello, this is Hardy Lee."

I felt my stomach drop, and a lump form in my throat. I had imagined that moment for years, ever since that early morning phone call when the truth first unraveled from my mom's friend. I had rehearsed what I would say. All the questions I would ask. All the things I needed to understand. But before I could even get past my stunned "Hello?" he spoke again.

"Look, I got your message. I'm not sure what your mother told you, but I don't know her. It sounds like she's playing a cruel trick on you, and for that I'm sorry. But I'm not your father. And I do not know your mother."

I tried to steady my voice and asked him to confirm a few basic pieces of information. And the way he answered, after my many years of deception detection and interrogation training, I knew he was lying. He gave me an easy out, an alternative story to cling to:

"Well, I dated a Spanish woman around that time.

Moved her to California.

But she wasn't Turkish.

So I don't know what else to tell you.

Please, don't contact me again."

I don't know what I thought would happen. Maybe some part of me imagined he'd recognize my voice, say he had been waiting for this moment too, or that he had spent years wondering about me. Maybe I thought there would be a kind of reunion you see in movies, awkward at first, then redemptive. But reality didn't come dressed in sentiment. It came like a locked door, closed before I could even knock.

People who lie often give just enough truth to camouflage the lie, a thread of similarity to ease their conscience and misdirect the listener. It was all too obvious. At that moment, I was flooded with emotions I struggled to name: Anger. Resentment. Rejection. Disbelief. And more anger, still. I hadn't even realized I had expectations. I hadn't realized how much I had hoped to be wanted. Not just known. Wanted. But whatever I had imagined, it wasn't this. And Hardy wasn't capable of giving it to me.

At first, indignation rose in me like armor. Well, if he doesn't want to acknowledge me, then to hell with him. But that wasn't the truth either. Beneath the anger was a much older ache. I was back under the bed again. A little girl. Scared. Ashamed. Rejected. The same darkness. The same silence. The same unanswered cry. Even in the rejection, God was clearing the ground. Some things fall away so the real work of healing can finally begin.

At that moment, I let go again, not because I wanted to but because I had no other choice. I was tired of begging for acceptance and validation. Tired of trying to belong. Tired of being unseen. I decided maybe that part of me, the part that longed to be claimed, was something God was keeping hidden. And He must have had a reason for it. I found peace in that surrender, but that didn't mean I stopped thinking about my real father. Or the life I had missed out on. I dreamed about how differently my childhood might have been. How differently my life might have played out. The abuse, the suffering, the constant survival mode, maybe none of it would have happened. Maybe I would have been whole. Maybe I would have been happy.

In an act of tender love, God whispered to the places no one else could reach: *You are already whole. You are already loved. You have always been Mine.*

It took years for that truth to root itself deep enough in me. And maybe, in my frail human understanding, I still don't fully grasp the depth of His love and grace. But in that moment, God was to me what He was to Hagar, a foreign single mother, desperately clinging to God's promise. He is El Roi: *The God who sees me.* In the unseen places, God was still working, setting things into motion I couldn't yet see.

Time passed. Life kept moving. But even in the quiet, the question lingered. Was Hardy really my dad? Some days I barely noticed it. Other days it hummed underneath everything like a song I couldn't quite silence. I'd catch a glimpse of my son Jacob's profile or the shape of his mouth when he concentrated, and I'd wonder if it matched his grandfather's, if it matched Hardy's. Sometimes I prayed, not for reunion, just for peace. For release. For whatever closure God saw fit to give. And then, He did.

Seven years later, through AncestryDNA, I received a connection update that linked me directly to a man I learned was Hardy's cousin. It was the first tangible proof, undeniable DNA evidence that connected me to the family I had been searching for. With cautious hope, I reached out to him through Ancestry's messaging system, explaining who I was and asking if he could help me contact Hardy. Maybe, I thought, if Hardy saw the truth in black and white, he would finally acknowledge me.

To my surprise, he responded. For the first time, hope flickered where only rejection had lived before. He was open to hearing my story and offered to share information about Hardy. I replied immediately, over-flowing with gratitude and anticipation. But then, silence. Days passed. Then weeks. My hope, so fragile and fleeting, withered in that silence. It was painful, but not unfamiliar. I had learned long ago what it felt like to be left unanswered. A month later, a message finally came, but not from him and not on Ancestry. It was a private Facebook message from Sean, Hardy's son. My brother.

As I stared at the screen, my pulse pounded with equal parts fear and hope. Would he ask me again to leave them alone? Would he dismiss me as some crazy stranger clinging to a fantasy? His words shattered every-thing. He told me that Hardy had died just two months prior. And then, the apology. The confession. I could tell it wasn't easy for him to write. That kind of truth takes courage. The kind that costs something.

Sean explained that when I had first reached out to him years ago, he had asked Hardy directly. And Hardy had assured him I was just some delusional woman harassing him. But now, faced with the truth, Sean admitted that deep down, he had always suspected I was telling the truth. He just hadn't been ready to face what that truth would mean. Now, he was ready. He wanted to talk. He wanted to tell me about Hardy. To share pieces of the father I never got to know. To answer the questions I had been carrying for forty-two years.

As I read his message, I felt the blood rush through my veins, as if every cell in my body had awakened at once. The familiar emotions returned and erupted. Anger. Sorrow. Resentment. Confusion. All swirling together in a storm I had been holding back for a lifetime. For so long, I had searched for acknowledgement. For answers. And now, in the wake of Hardy's death, the truth had finally found its way to me. But it came too late.

We exchanged several messages back and forth. Sean told me how Hardy died, and I answered some questions he had. He sent me pictures, one of him and his brother, my other brother, sitting next to that bronze

Porsche. And photos of Hardy as a young man, from the early eighties, around the time he likely met my mother. I looked at Hardy in that photo, and I saw my face. I stared at it, studying every detail. It felt surreal, like looking through time and seeing my reflection in someone else. His brow. My eyes. Jacob's bone structure. It was like finding a missing line in a poem I had been reciting my whole life. A puzzle piece I had stopped searching for, thinking maybe it never existed. But there it was, clear as day, legacy. I saw Jacob in his grandfather.

There is something lonely about being the odd one out. Sure, I looked like my mother, but she was absent from most of my life. There had always been a sense that something was missing, a missing piece to the puzzle. And after years of wondering, there it was. I looked a lot like him, Hardy. I have the same deep brown eyes. The same long legs and short torso. And so does Jacob. It was all so sad and so beautiful at the same time. For the first time in my life, I, in a sense, belonged.

Sean asked if he could set up a time to have a real conversation. There were things he wanted to tell me, things that deserved more than a few messages. At the very least, they deserved a phone call. It was kind of him; as much as I was feeling, I couldn't imagine what he must have been going through, too. We started following each other on social media. He liked a picture I posted of my Corvette and teased that it wasn't as fast as his yellow Porsche GT3, but it was nice. Then he added, *"I guess the apple doesn't fall far from the tree after all."*

And in that small olive branch of an exchange, Sean and I found common ground, and the beginnings of a bridge over so much pain and so many years of lost time.

CHAPTER 14

Can You See the Rain?

I WOKE UP early on a Saturday morning, a little after four a.m., to a thunderstorm. I went to use the bathroom, and I could hear the gusts of wind and the rain pounding against the house. I knew, because of what I heard, that it was windy and raining outside, but I didn't see it yet. I couldn't feel the rain on my skin or the wind through my hair. But I heard it. And with it came the quiet refrain of a truth I had learned by heart, that even when the storm raged, there was a foundation beneath me that could not be shaken. I was wide awake by then, so I went and sat quietly on the chaise by the large living room window facing the backyard. It was my sacred place, where I met with the Lord every morning, reading, praying, and listening for His voice.

It had been a long, emotional week of writing this memoir, and my heart was so heavy. I believed God was calling me to do this, a work of healing and freedom, not only for myself but for others weighed down by shame and guilt. However, fear started creeping in. I knew I had heard God clearly; I heard the promise to bless this work, to break generational cycles, and to bring prosperity and restoration to my family. I knew His voice. I knew His promises. But when I looked around and struggled through the darkness I was hidden in, the fruit of His Word and the evidence of His promise were unseen, and I became discouraged.

That morning, as I stayed there in silence, staring through the window, the world outside looked dark, heavy, and blurred, a thick, almost invisible veil pressing against the glass. At first glance, it didn't even seem like it was raining, just darkness swallowing everything. Then a car passed by on the road behind my fence. The high beams from its headlights caught the falling rain and suddenly, what I hadn't seen before was revealed. The rain had been falling the entire time.

As I looked closer, I noticed the trees beginning to sway, their limbs moving, dancing, carried by a wind blowing. And God spoke to my spirit:

In the darkest hours, when you cannot see clearly, when everything feels uncertain, stay focused on Me, remember what I told you. Even when your eyes cannot see, the rain of My promises is already falling.

Even when you cannot feel it, My Spirit is moving. The winds of change are already at work.

Even though I had heard the rain battering my house, when I first looked outside, all I saw was darkness. But when I stayed at the window, watching, waiting, trusting, the headlights revealed what had been hidden: the rain. The trees bent in the wind. The movement of a Spirit that had never stopped working. Then lightning flashed, the sky split open, and with it came an unmistakable reminder: Even when your senses fail you, My Word remains true.

Back then, I didn't have the language for what I was feeling. All I knew was a strange pull, a whisper I kept trying to make sense of. I kept asking God for something I could see, something I could hold onto. Maybe that's why the question echoed in me long before I ever understood it: *Can you see the rain?*

I realize now that much of this story has focused on the brokenness, and while that's an honest part of my journey, it's not the whole story. The most important part happened when I gave my life to Jesus. I was 12, almost 13. Still a little girl but already carrying wounds far too heavy for my small shoulders. I didn't understand everything about faith. I didn't know all the theology or have the right words. I wasn't concerned with my immortal soul; I was just trying to escape the hell I was living in. The church did that much for me.

I often found it difficult to believe the words coming out of our Jesus-look-alike pastor, Roger. His words were clear and anointed: they were words that my dad and Norma and the congregation applauded loudly but denied with the way they lived behind closed doors. Sometimes, we didn't even make it out of the church parking lot before the yelling and fighting began.

If the Bible was so important, if Jesus was so important, why was He only ever mentioned on Sundays and Wednesdays when we went to church? Was God like a parent with restrictive visitation rights, only allowed on Sundays and Wednesdays? Even so, I was happy at church. I kind of had friends, though I never really felt understood by them and wasn't really allowed to hang out with them outside of church events, but I liked it there.

As for Jesus, I didn't grow up in Sunday school. I wasn't raised with the faith of a mustard seed fed by stories of David and Goliath, or Daniel in the lion's den. It all sounded like fairy tales, and by that age, I had already stopped believing in fairy tales. But I was curious. And I think God can do something with a curious and open heart.

The important part was that I was hearing the Word of God, little puzzle pieces scattered across the table. None of it made much sense yet, but God was working behind the scenes.

It was a Wednesday morning, trash day, when I was young. My sister and I were responsible for taking four large, usually overflowing trash cans down the long gravel driveway to the service road where we caught the school bus. We weren't allowed to drag the cans on the gravel road; it would wear holes in the bottoms of the trash cans. So, we dragged them across the patchy grass, if you want to call it that. It was just acres of weeds, mowed and weed-eaten by yours truly.

The trash cans didn't have wheels, and they were heavy. We couldn't lift them, even when we tried, so we would end up with garbage juice spilling on us, and nobody wants to smell like garbage at school. Eventually, our dad got us a couple of dollies, and we would stack the trash cans and wheel them down to the service road.

My sister Pamela wasn't exactly mean, but she often knowingly and unknowingly used her "real daughter" privilege. If she got there first, she would take both dollies, stack her trash cans, and leave me with none. That morning, I was running a little late getting ready for school and the bus was coming soon, so I knew there would be hell to pay if I missed the bus. I didn't have time to wait for Pamela to return the dollies, So I dragged them across the "grass" in the front yard.

Norma, already in one of her moods, caught me about halfway down the front yard dragging the trash cans. Pamela was already on her way back with the dollies when Norma snapped. She burst outside screaming and cussing at both of us. And for the first time that I recall, Pamela, who rarely spoke up, shouted back, *"This is so stupid! Who cares about the trash cans?!"* Norma slapped her. Hard. I was stunned. I was used to being hit. But Pamela? I had never seen that before.

What happened next haunted me for years. Without hesitation, Pamela dropped the dollies and slapped Norma back. It was as if the world had stopped spinning on its axis and everything stood still. I thought Norma was going to kill her. I ran between them, yelling for Norma to leave her alone. Norma turned on me, screaming, "You want some of this, too?" Pamela and I ran inside and slammed our bedroom doors. Dad heard the chaos and came to find out what happened. He talked to Pamela first, then told us both to get in the truck. He would drive us to school.

After school, Pamela stayed in her room and I stayed in mine; it was safer that way. About thirty minutes later, Pamela came to my room and told me it was time for dinner. I asked her what had happened. She told me, with disbelief, that Norma had come into her room crying and apologized. Norma. Apologizing. But then the reality hit harder: Norma apologized to Pamela, not to me. Not ever to me. And to make matters worse, I was grounded and forbidden from going to Bible camp that weekend, punished for dragging the trash cans and "talking back." Pamela wasn't punished at all; it wasn't her fault. But in a way, I was proud of her for her bravery.

However, another part of me resented her. I resented the way she was protected while I was left exposed. I resented the way she never spoke up for me the way I had just stood up for her. I was alone and defenseless in that house. No sister. No church members. No one standing in the gap for me.

Once, I even threatened to call the police because of the treatment. My dad handed me the phone and said, *"Go ahead. But just know what's coming as soon as you do. I won't be falsely accused."* The message was clear: If I dared to tell, he would make sure I had something real to tell.

That evening, we still went to church. I don't remember what the youth pastor preached about; I was too numb. But I do remember him saying that Christ was our refuge. Our shelter in times of trouble. And I needed that more than anything. I walked to the front and accepted Jesus as my Savior. The lights felt too bright. My hands trembled. I didn't know what to say, but I whispered something anyway, something like, "Please help." I don't know if anyone else heard it, but I know Heaven did.

It wasn't a moment of profound revelation. It wasn't because I understood doctrine or redemption. It was desperation. It was survival. Clinging to anything that might save me. He didn't rescue me from the abuse, not then. But a seed was planted. Quiet. Hidden. Alive. Buried deep in the soil of a little girl's heart. It would take years before that faith would break through the hardened layers of shame, fear, survival, and striving. But the seed was there. Alive. Growing even when I couldn't see it. Even when I wandered. Even when I doubted. Even when I buried myself in survival and forgot how to hope, God never left me.

Hear me when I say this: I do not believe God allows suffering for suffering's sake. But I do believe He brings purpose out of every ounce of our pain. God had a purpose for my life while I grew in the womb of a woman who wanted to discard me. He knew the empathy and compassion born from survival. He knew I would be a mother, one who had walked through fire and would fiercely guard the hearts of her children. God knew I would need to be the voice I never had, the one who stands up and says, *"No, you're not going to hurt them."*

I wasn't just trained to be a highly skilled soldier in the Army. Before all of that, God was arming me with His Word, His Spirit, and my own story. He was forging a warrior for the voiceless. A protector of the marginalized. An advocate for the broken. God wrote my story way before I sat down to write this memoir. He knew the same healing hands that set me free would reach out through these pages and set others free, too.

I was not just saved for myself; no one is. I was saved so others could be, too. And that is the kind of story only God can write. The God who had called me to Himself at twelve years old, the God who had whispered over the chaos of my childhood, the God who had planted a promise in the dark. He was the same God who sat with me, years later, at that window in the dark. In the fog. Still speaking. Still leading. Still keeping every promise He ever made.

I didn't know it back then, at twelve years old, when I first said yes to Jesus. I didn't know it when I wandered through years of confusion, clinging to survival instead of hope. I didn't know it when I searched the skies begging for a sign, a voice, a reason. But sitting by the window years later, I see it with clarity: The rain has always been falling. The Spirit has always been moving. The promises have always been there, even when my visibility was too clouded.

And maybe the question was never, *"Can you see the rain?"* Maybe the better question was: *"Can you trust that it is falling even when you couldn't see it?"*

CHAPTER 15

Forgiveness Without Apology

AFTER ALL THE pain, betrayals, and silent wounds, I learned something that changed everything: Forgiveness is rarely clean. It doesn't arrive on time or come tied up with a bow. More often, it shows up when no apology ever does. It whispers when closure is silent, and it demands more from us than justice ever will.

I spent much of my life waiting for apologies that never came, from my mother, from my dad, from Hardy, from Timothy, from my sister. I thought I needed their acknowledgment to be free, but I have come to understand that freedom doesn't come when someone says sorry; it comes when I surrender the need for it. I forgave Hardy, not because he deserved it but because carrying his denial was poisoning my peace. I forgave my dad, not the man I wanted him to be but the wounded man he truly was. I forgave my mother, not the version I created in my childhood dreams but the complex, often damaged woman who tried her best with what she had. I forgave Timothy, not because he ever recognized his part in the destruction of our marriage but because I refused to let bitterness chain me to a story God had already redeemed. I forgave my sister, not because she stood by me when I needed her most but because my healing could not wait for her understanding.

And I forgave myself, which was the hardest of all, for the affairs, for the lies, for the manipulation, for the self-deception, for the judgment I once cast on others. In those moments, I never knew I would wear shame like a second skin. I forgave the woman I used to be, the one who made decisions from fear, from desperation, from wounds that hadn't yet healed. This kind of forgiveness is holy; it is fierce. It is not a feeling; it's a choice, a spiritual discipline. And it is the key that opened the door to the legacy I now fight to leave behind for my sons. I am not perfect, but I am no longer angry, no longer bitter, no longer demanding to be made whole by people who couldn't even heal themselves. I have been forgiven by the only One who matters, and because of that, I can forgive those who never asked for it. But forgiveness isn't a one-time act; it is something I have to choose again and again, especially in the seasons that test my resilience.

Spring of 2020 arrived, and everything had shut down due to COVID. I couldn't work at first but thank God He provided. I had just been awarded a veterans' disability benefit, and it was enough to carry us through that season. The boys were out of school, and we did what we could to pass the time during the most restrictive part of the lockdown. Texas wasn't nearly as bad as most states, but it was still tough on us all economically.

I was renting a small home close to the boys' school, trying to keep up with all the essentials: bills, utilities, car payments, groceries, rent. Timothy paid child support at the time, but it was a small amount I had agreed to when we initially divorced, based on his circumstances then. He had been between jobs, and the agreement included a promise to help more when needed. But like any good attorney will tell you, if it's not in writing, it's as if it never happened.

To say we struggled was an understatement. I had just come off the high of successfully competing in a bodybuilding show in December 2019, having completely transformed my body. Hoping to build on that momentum, I began taking online courses to become a certified personal trainer and nutrition coach. I attempted to create income in a season where opportunity was scarce. The gym owner who had promised me a job once the gyms reopened generously lent me equipment so I could train at home, make content for clients, and stay visible on social media. Back then, I was known as @mj_fitmom. A few of my clients began seeing results, and it gave me hope. However, starting out as a personal trainer rarely brings in consistent income.

We were barely staying afloat. I missed a rent payment and had to juggle which bills to pay just to keep the utilities on and food in the fridge. When I explained my situation to the landlord, they offered a brief extension. But even with the extra time, the math didn't add up. If I paid what I owed in full, we'd be left without heat, lights, or groceries. School was about to resume with an online option, but the digital learning platform was unreliable and nearly impossible to navigate.

I needed help. Not luxuries. Not handouts. Just help. And when I turned to my co-parent, Timothy, I was met with indifference wrapped in judgment instead of compassion and a willingness to support.

"You need to figure it out on your own. I pay child support," he said, as if those few dollars erased the needs of two growing boys. I tried to explain, tried to remind him that he was paying far less than what the courts would have required and that he had agreed to step in when needed.

"You should learn to manage that money better," he snapped back.

Meanwhile, the world was gasping under the weight of a pandemic. Families everywhere were tightening their belts just to survive. But not Timothy. He was flourishing, flashing a brand-new Mercedes, a brand-new GMC diesel truck, while I struggled to scrape together enough for school supplies and clothes that fit the boys' growing bodies.

At that point, we had been divorced for over five years. He had moved on, new relationships, new life, new luxury, and still he found ways to make co-parenting as difficult, as punishing, and as soul-squeezing as possible. And it wasn't just direct. It was indirect, almost calculated, as if he were standing off to the side, arms folded, watching and waiting for me to fail, not so he could step in and be a better father but so he could gossip about my struggle. So, he could poison the ears of anyone who would listen, masked in the tone of a "concerned parent." It wasn't about the boys. It wasn't about love. It was about control, about preserving the story where he looked strong and I looked weak.

When someone can no longer control you, they will try to control how others see you. Psychologist Dr. George Simon wrote extensively about covert-aggressive personalities. In his book, *In Sheep's Clothing*, he describes how manipulators attack your character when they can no longer control your life. Evolutionary studies at Stanford show that nearly 92% of human conversations about others are evaluative; we are not just relaying information, but are shaping perception. We are deciding, often unconsciously, if this person is safe or dangerous, good or bad.

In healthy communities, that instinct can protect the vulnerable. But in the hands of the wrong person, it becomes a weapon, a way to control the narrative when they can no longer control the person. And that's exactly what Timothy did.

Even though the justice system was supposed to protect families from eviction during the lockdowns of the pandemic, my landlord successfully evicted me. I will never forget the embarrassment as my neighbors and people driving by watched as the constable and staff removed me and my children's belongings from the house and onto the roadside. I had enough money to have those items put into storage and to pay for us to stay in a hotel room for a bit. It was undoubtedly the biggest failure of my life.

Even though I swore I would never turn to my dad and Norma for help, the boys and I were in a dangerous and desperate situation. I had to swallow my pride and take any criticism that might follow asking for help. Dad and Norma and I were not really on good speaking terms, so I knew the hell that would follow asking for their help, but I had to do something. I reached out to them to see if we could stay in one of their mobile homes or their mother-in-law apartment until I could get us back on our feet.

Norma responded sharply and quickly: "No, the rent we get from the trailers is part of our income. You cannot stay here." They offered to pay for a few more nights of our hotel stay, but I declined their help because I was so humiliated and angry.

They had reached out to my sister. She called me, angry that I had not told her what was going on and that I didn't ask for help, angry that I let my situation get this bad. I just took everything she said, every judgment, because she was right. Why didn't I ask her for help? If the first few chapters didn't paint the picture vividly enough, we were raised to figure things out on our own. The world wasn't going to save us; our family wasn't going to save us. We had to figure it out.

After Pamela was done scolding me, she talked to her husband, and they offered to pay for another week of hotel stay. Places started to open back up, and I was able to get a part-time job as a technician at Cryotherapy.

The money wasn't much, but it was enough to start saving. I also became good friends with the staff there and reconnected with my friend, Angie. She helped me get the job, and my sweet friend, Jessica, through her family loss and grieving, found herself in a four-bedroom family home alone and offered to let the boys and I stay there with her until we could save more money and get back on our feet.

When I tell you that God moves, I mean it with every bit of sincerity I can muster. God moved on my behalf. He didn't make things easy on me, but He was teaching me to come to Him with my burdens and my fears and listen to His voice, that He would provide. And He always did.

I was able to save enough money and get into a nice home. Unfortunately, even though God showed me He would care for me and my family and that I could depend on Him, I still looked for opportunities to manipulate and make things happen on my own. That default of self-preservation at any cost is not easily destroyed. I did what I could to secure a new home, all the while taking Timothy to court for an increase in child support. The battle dragged on for over two years; his lawyer filed continuance after continuance, draining me of any money that I had tried to save. This again put me in a position where I didn't have enough money to pay for my home or my car. I was drifting on a raft of deception, constantly anxious, knowing it would eventually collapse beneath me.

But God was still present, still protecting my family, even in my mess and mistakes. That is what a loving Father does. He doesn't withhold correction, but He never turns His back on you. That was something I never knew growing up. Love and compassion were conditional, transactional. But not with God. He saw through the lies, the desperation, and kept pursuing my heart because He had something better waiting for me, something I couldn't yet see.

After a long battle with Timothy in court, I sat through his testimony where he painted me as a terrible mother, spinning lies about how I neglected the boys, twisting every failure into proof that I was unfit. But the judge saw right through it.

She asked him, "If you really believed your children were being neglected and not cared for, why did you only wait to bring this up when she brought you here for an increase in child support? If you saw and knew she was struggling, why didn't you help her when she asked?"

Timothy and his lawyer offered no explanation grounded in truth or genuine concern, and the judge saw right through it. She ordered the state's maximum child support, more than double what he had been paying, and granted back pay to my original filing nearly two years earlier. It was an incredible relief: I was able to do something special for the boys, catch up on overdue bills, and, for the first time in a long time, exhale. But the ruling only fueled Timothy's rage. And with Timothy, there was always a plan brewing beneath the surface.

He had already done so much damage to my reputation through gossip and manipulation that I became isolated from my own community, the very hometown where I grew up. That isolation left lasting effects I still feel today. Even my sister and her husband sided with him for a time. As lonely and painful as that season was, I held tightly to the truth of Romans 8:31: *"If God is for me, who can stand against me?"*

The court ruling wasn't just a financial hit for Timothy; it struck his ego. And I still feel the aftershocks. Eventually, I chose to forgive him because I refused to let my children grow up in a home defined by conflict. They deserved peace, love, and a sense of safety, not the confusion of constant tension.

It is something I must ask God for the strength to do almost daily. And God often reminds me that Timothy is His child, too. That God loves him. When you strengthen the muscle of emotional maturity, you begin to see that the way people treat you says more about them than it does about you. Their words and actions are often a reflection of their own pain and inner struggle. We become mirrors, and when someone looks at us and doesn't like what they see reflected, they lash out.

There is nothing I can do to make Timothy forgive me for the things I did in the past, and nothing I can do to make him apologize for the things he did, or the way he still treats me. But I chose to forgive him anyway.

Jesus told a parable about this kind of mercy. A king forgave a servant's massive, unpayable debt, only to watch that same servant choke and imprison another man over a tiny amount he was owed. When the king heard what happened, he was outraged. "I canceled all that debt of yours because you begged me to. Shouldn't you have had mercy on your fellow servant just as I had on you?" That is the kingdom Jesus invites us to live in.

Forgiveness is not optional. It is not contingent on an apology. Forgiveness does not rewrite the past, but it clears the path forward for anyone who has ever had to heal. It is the standard Jesus set for those who have been forgiven much. And I have been forgiven a lot. So, I choose to forgive, even when it costs me, even when it hurts, even when there is no apology, and especially then. But forgiveness does not mean forgetting. It does not mean pretending the harm never happened or welcoming someone back into your life without accountability. Forgiveness is about freedom, not access. I can release someone from the debt they owe me without letting them back into the sacred places of my life.

Boundaries can be tricky for Christ-followers. We are called to break down some boundaries and reach out to others, but it is healthy to erect boundaries to protect us from physical or spiritual harm. Boundaries are not un-Christian; they are protection. Forgiveness brings us peace, but proper boundaries keep us safe to thrive. I can love someone from a distance. I can pray for them without picking up where we left off. That is not bitterness but wisdom.

CHAPTER 16

Is This Love?

HEALING DOES NOT come wrapped in a bow. It does not arrive all at once as a finished gift from Heaven. It comes in battles, in choices, in long nights where the only thing holding you together is the whisper of a promise you cannot yet see.

When I decided to take my relationship with the Lord seriously, it was not some magical, "bippity boppity boo" transformation. My scars did not evaporate. My old patterns did not vanish overnight. The old wounds still bled when touched, and the old voices still whispered when I least expected them.

And nowhere was that fight more visible than in the battlefield of modern dating. For women like me, who carried childhood wounds like hidden landmines, modern dating is more than confusing; it is warfare. They call it "talking" now, the stage where someone dates multiple people but minimizes it by saying it's nothing serious; they're just "talking." Just enough intimacy to stir hope, just enough distance to avoid responsibility.

Modern dating activates something deep in a woman with low self-worth, the need to compete, to be chosen, to prove her value. You are made to feel "crazy" for asking for clarity, "needy" for wanting commitment, and "too much" for wanting to know where you stand. And if you dare to set a boundary, you are quickly replaced, proof, they imply, that you were never worth choosing in the first place.

For someone like me, whose wounds ran deep and leaned toward anxious attachment, it was a perfect storm. Anxious attachment doesn't simply want love; it needs reassurance like oxygen. Every delayed text, every vague answer, every canceled plan felt like confirmation of the fear I had carried since childhood: that I was not enough to be loved consistently.

Meanwhile, the men I found myself drawn to often operated with avoidant attachment, thriving on pursuit but retreating the moment emotional intimacy demanded anything real. It was a cruel dance: I chased; they withdrew. I gave; they disappeared. I begged to be seen; they looked through me. Without realizing it, I kept accepting breadcrumbs, believing they were the feast my heart had been longing for.

But it went deeper than just attachment styles. It was not just about dating but about me trying, over and over, to convince someone who was not capable of giving me the love I so desperately craved to somehow give it anyway. I subconsciously wanted them to be the father I never had, the husband I never had, the protector and safe place my soul had ached for since childhood. I wanted them to prove to me that even though my past was riddled with mistakes, I was still worthy of being loved, still worthy of being chosen, still worthy of being cherished.

Each cycle of heartbreak revealed something God was trying to show me all along: the kind of love I was searching for, the kind that heals, that covers, that challenges, that makes you feel seen and safe does not come from broken people. It can only come from God.

I lived that. Over and over. I "talked" to men who were charming, attentive, and promised the world until boundaries were placed. One man wanted a relationship early on but only because he needed a distraction from his own brokenness. He pushed for intimacy early, and even though I protested at first, I gave in. Another was a flashy real-estate agent who loved fast cars like me. He took me to concerts, fancy dinners, and bought expensive gifts for my sons and me, all the while making plans. Turns out his divorce really wasn't finished. He was still begging for her to forgive him for cheating and to take him back, while he was dating me and sleeping with other very young women. As soon as I raised questions and communicated boundaries, I was dismissed as needy and crazy.

I kept asking God, "Is it me? Do I only attract this?" But the truth was I hadn't yet learned to believe I was worth more.

Another was a musician I had known since high school, now living the dream life as a guitar player. He pursued me with so much kindness and admiration, only to push hard for physical intimacy early on. Again, I gave in. Again, I was discarded soon after.

Another came from my Corvette car club: handsome, attentive, love-bombing me with chivalry and affection. But beneath it all, he was just looking for exactly what the other men were. Access, not responsibility.

Then there was my old battle buddy from the Army. We had served in a combat zone together. There was chemistry, as he was attractive, funny, and strong. Recently divorced and sprinting through the rebound circuit, he wasn't looking for depth, faith, or anything resembling real connection. Something in me shifted. I realized I didn't want another relationship that drained me or kept me small. I was tired. I was done. I didn't want to date at all, not for a long while.

In this time, I needed to learn how to sit in the singleness, to let the quiet do its work. To be content in my own skin. I needed space for God to mend the parts of me I kept handing to the wrong men. And when I'm whole, and ready, I trust He'll bring someone who loves Him and knows how to love me the way I was designed to be loved. For the first time in my life, I chose the dry phone and the lonely nights over the quick fix of temporary affection. I chose God's promises over the world's counterfeits. In the silence that followed, I began to reclaim something deeper than control and more like communion.

Some mornings I would sit in stillness with worship music playing low, my Bible open but unread, tears in my eyes for reasons I couldn't name. Healing didn't look like a dramatic deliverance. It looked like showing up. It looked like letting God hold the parts of me I still didn't understand.

It took me longer than I like to admit to fully understand that no man, no matter how charming or beautiful or broken, could ever offer me the healing my soul needed. Only God could do that. And He was waiting, patiently, lovingly, for me to finally stop chasing shadows and turn to Him.

Since then, I've had no desire to "talk" to just anyone. I've been asked out. Opportunities have come. But there's no need to prove myself worthy of being chosen. Because I already am. I am chosen by the One who sees me fully and loves me wholly. This transformation is a battle. A daily choice to believe that what God has for me is worth the wait, even when it costs me comfort. Even when it leaves me feeling alone. Even when the enemy whispers that I'm missing out. But I'm not missing out. I'm being protected. I'm being preserved. I'm being prepared. Because the love story God is writing for me in His timing, in His way, will be one that honors everything He has healed in me. And I would rather wait in faith than settle in fear. "Wait for the Lord; be strong, and let your heart take courage; wait for the Lord" (Psalm 27:14).

CHAPTER 17

For the Ones After Me

HEALING IN LOVE was never just about me. It wasn't simply about finding the right man or learning how to be chosen for the right reasons. It was about breaking a cycle that was bigger than me, a cycle that stretched back through generations of wounds, silence, and survival. God was not just healing my heart for my sake. He was healing me for the sake of the ones coming after me. For the sons I was raising. For the legacy I would leave behind. Because real healing always ripples outward.

I wanted to stop the bleeding. I wanted my sons to grow up in truth, not silence. To be raised in grace, not guilt. To see repentance modeled, not perfection demanded. I wanted them to know a version of love that didn't come with fear or shame attached to it. That meant tending to my own wounds, telling the truth even when I didn't look good in it, and becoming the kind of woman I wanted my sons to trust, not just obey.

I know I didn't always get it right; I failed more times than I wanted to. But I also know I didn't give up. And now, I pray they will remember their mother as a woman who faced her demons, asked for help, walked with Jesus, and did not let her past define her future.

I already see the fruit of that surrender in them. I see it in the way they ask questions without fear. In the way they pray out loud without shame. In the way they come to me with their hearts wide open, expecting to be heard, not punished.

Once, one of them asked, "Mom, do you think I'll be a good dad someday?"

Without hesitation, I said yes. Not because I've been a perfect example, but because I've given them something true. Because I've stayed. I've grown. I'm healing. And they've seen every part of it. They are learning how to build something new and better.

Keeping boundaries and upholding God's standards can feel like you're building a wall that separates you from everyone else, when really you're building an altar. I didn't learn that in peace. I learned it in loneliness. I spent time drawing closer to the Lord, getting to know His voice, and letting Him expose all the ways I was chasing after relationships that bore no fruit. Relationships that filled time but emptied me.

The spiritual warfare didn't stop just because I finally walked away from sin and shame, because the devil doesn't walk away just because you did. And progress? It doesn't always look linear, and sometimes it feels like pressure. Like isolation. Like silence. But that's when God does His deepest work, beneath the surface, in the soil, where roots grow strong long before the fruit ever appears. That's where trust is born. Not in the spotlight, but in the stillness.

And when I think about how far He's brought me, I'm reminded that some of the most powerful seeds of transformation were planted in moments I didn't even realize were sacred. Sometimes it takes looking back years later to finally see what God was doing. One of those moments came long before I had language for what God was doing in me.

I've been thinking a lot about a moment that happened nearly twenty-one years ago. My good friend, James, from high school, was the drummer in a band that happened to be on tour near my city in Virginia. He invited me to come see them. I left for the Army right after high school and had no idea that some of my friends from back home had landed a major record deal and were touring all over the world. James left me passes at will call, and I went to hang out backstage with the rest of the band, Flyleaf.

It was surreal. There's a special kind of joy in watching people you care about walk in the blessings God has for them. It's humbling and beautiful to see what He can do in someone's life.

While other bands were performing, Lacey, their lead vocalist, asked if she could talk to me privately. She said she had something important she wanted to share, something I've never forgotten, even if it's taken me two decades to fully understand what God was really saying through her.

She told me a story about a little girl who clung tightly to a cheap set of fake pearls she believed had belonged to her late mother. The pearls were her most prized possession, her link to the only love she had ever known. Her father, knowing the truth, would come to her at bedtime and gently ask, "Will you give me those pearls?" And each time, the little girl would refuse. "They are all I have left of her," she would say. Her father didn't argue; he just waited. A few days later, he asked again. "Please, daughter, trust me. They are not real, but I have something better for you." Again, she refused. Again, he didn't push. He just waited until she was ready.

One night, with trembling hands and tear-filled eyes, she finally said, "Okay, Daddy. I trust you," and gave him the pearls she had held onto so tightly for so long. He embraced her with joy and told her to wait patiently. And not long after, he gave her a beautiful, blue velvet box with the most beautiful, rare, priceless pearls, the very ones her mother had worn in the photo on her bedside table.

That night, Lacey looked me in the eye and said, "God says you are holding on to things that are not real. Cheap imitations. But when you are ready to surrender, He will give you everything He promised."

It has taken me twenty-one years to understand that moment. To look back and see how many times I clung to things, not because they were good but because they were familiar. Because I believed they were all I had. I see now that God has been asking me, gently and patiently, "Will you give this to Me? It is not real. But I promise, I have something better."

Now, I am ready to let go.

The anger, the resentment, the trauma, the need for control, the striving, they are falling away. Not all at once, but like layers peeling back as I step into who God has always seen me as.

For the women like me who are still holding tightly to broken things, not realizing their hands are too full to receive what is real. I see it now. God did not ask me to let go to leave me empty. He asked me to let go so He could fill me with something priceless. Something real. And He is doing it. "I will give you hidden treasures, riches stored in secret places, so that you may know that I am the Lord, the God of Israel, who summons you by name" (Isaiah 45:3).

CHAPTER 18

The Hour After Sehar

THE HOUR OF Sehar is beautiful, holy, and unforgettable. But it leaves behind a haunting question: What do I do now? For many new believers and for those who have wrestled long with their faith, this may feel like the finish line. Yet the truth is, it is only the beginning. Transformation is not an event; it is a daily, humbling, often painful process. It is the story of, "I am a broken person, loved by a perfect God, being led through healing." And it is slow, often hidden, often hard.

Philosophy helped name how our inner frameworks are formed. Psychology helped explain how those frameworks fracture under trauma and attachment wounds. But the missing piece, the one neither discipline could fully supply, was spirituality and theology: not as a substitute for understanding or healing, but as the force that tears down what is broken and rebuilds it in alignment with who we were always meant to be. Healing, I came to see, happens at the intersection, where philosophy, psychology, and faith meet, inform one another, and work together toward wholeness.

Philosophers have wrestled for centuries with the mystery of the human mind. In his seventeenth-century work *An Essay Concerning Human Understanding*, John Locke famously proposed that we are born as a *tabula rasa*, a blank slate, written on only by the experiences of life.

According to Locke, nurture was everything. We become who we are through the impressions the world leaves on us, through every bruise, every kindness, every scar.[1]

But then came Immanuel Kant, who challenged that view. In *Critique of Pure Reason*, Kant believed we aren't born as empty canvases at all. He argued that we come into the world already carrying invisible structures inside us, built-in frameworks that shape how we see, feel, and understand long before experience ever touches us. According to Kant, perception itself is filtered through these deep frameworks. Our minds don't just passively absorb the world; they interpret it. They organize it. They name it, even before we have language.

Even before we learn the words for sorrow or safety, our hearts already *know* what they are. We *know* safety in the warmth of a mother's arms. We *know* it in the cold withdrawal of anger in a room. We *know* sorrow in the ache of absence when someone leaves who should have stayed.

These aren't just lessons life teaches us; they're categories our souls seem wired to recognize. Before we can speak the word *trust*, we're already attuned to safety or danger. Before we can define *betrayal*, we feel the sting of broken connection. This hidden architecture within us, what philosophers like Kant called innate structures of understanding, reveals something profound: Our deepest frameworks for love, fear, belonging, and rejection are sown into us long before memory ever takes root.

Psychological theories about how the mind develops often reflect these same philosophical debates. Sigmund Freud, often called the father of psychoanalysis, took the conversation inward. In works like *The Interpretation of Dreams* and his later psychoanalytic lectures, Freud argued that early childhood experiences, especially those inside our families, leave deep and lasting marks on the unconscious mind. Marks that don't just disappear as we grow up but silently shape our emotional lives in ways we often don't even realize.

Then Erik Erikson added another layer. In *Childhood and Society*, he proposed that human development doesn't happen all at once; it unfolds

---

1   John Locke's An Essay Concerning Human Understanding (1689), particularly Book II, Chapter I

in stages. Our innate drives and the world around us collide and weave together to build the architecture of who we are.

Even today, modern psychology still echoes what philosophers like Locke and Kant wrestled with centuries ago: Our minds are neither blank slates nor fixed destinies. They are living stories shaped by both what we inherit and what we experience. From our very first breaths, the seen and unseen forces swirling around us and inside us begin to form the narratives we carry. Stories about who we are. Stories about what love means. Stories about what it takes to be safe, to be wanted, to survive. Some of those stories are beautiful. Some of them are broken. But all of them start shaping us long before we even know they're there.

Philosophy and psychology affirm that our early frameworks shape how we see the world, and Scripture reveals an even deeper truth: We aren't just shaped by experience. We are born into brokenness. We inherit a corrupted framework, a fracture that distorts how we see ourselves, how we see others, and how we see God. King David wrote it plainly in the Psalms: "Surely I was sinful at birth, sinful from the time my mother conceived me" (Psalm 51:5, NIV). We aren't born blank or neutral. We come into the world already carrying the cracks of generations before us, what Scripture calls "the sins of the fathers" (Exodus 20:5). We start the race limping. We start the story already needing rescue.

But the beauty of the gospel, the breathtaking hope of Jesus, is that He doesn't just offer knowledge to patch our cracks. He offers transformation that rebuilds the foundation itself. When Jesus speaks about being "born again" (John 3:3–7), He isn't just talking about tweaking behaviors or making better choices. He's talking about a complete rebirth, a rewriting of the corrupted frameworks we've inherited. This brand-new beginning doesn't originate from our own strength but takes place deep within us as God's Spirit does His work. And Paul, echoing that same call, urges us to be "transformed by the renewing of your mind" (Romans 12:2). Not a one-time emotional high. Not a Sunday-only surface change. But a daily, ongoing reconstruction of how we think, how we believe, how we see.

Through Christ, the old, broken frameworks aren't just covered up; they're dismantled. And in their place, something eternal, something unshakable, begins to rise. In this way, God's Word serves both as mirror and blueprint: it exposes the fractures in the structures we've inherited, and it guides the rebuilding process on a foundation that cannot be shaken. Jesus illustrates this kind of transformation in the parable of the wise and foolish builders: "Everyone who hears these words of mine and puts them into practice is like a wise man who built his house on the rock" (Matthew 7:24, NIV).

But those who build their lives on shifting sands eventually find that when the storms come, everything collapses. Emotions fade. Traditions buckle. What once seemed trustworthy is revealed to be unworthy of trust.

There are still moments when my mind forgets the new foundation and falls back into the old ways and the battles that follow. Transformation doesn't happen in theory: it happens in the ordinary, frustrating, messy moments of real life—the school pick-up lines, the emails, the conversations that don't go the way you planned. And that's exactly where God met me one spring afternoon.

It was a spring Friday afternoon, a cool wind was blowing, and the sun was out. A perfect day to pick up Alex, my third-grader, from school in the Corvette, or "Blue Falcon," as he affectionately calls her. (Those of you who have been in the military will grin a little at that.)

I pulled into the pick-up line looking like I had just rolled out of bed, messy hair, hoodie, glasses, taking a break from writing this very memoir to come get him. The line wasn't any longer than usual, but maybe there was a little excitement in the air. It was Friday, the weather was perfect, and everyone just seemed a little lighter.

I understand the chaos that is the school drop-off and pick-up line, so I can sympathize with the stress teachers feel trying to navigate little elementary kids and impatient cars all at once. As I approached the front, where Alex usually would have range-walked (that's like a very fast-paced mall walk) to the car, a smiling teacher informed me that Alex hadn't come out yet and asked if I could park and wait.

"Sure, no problem at all," I told her. I checked my mirror, didn't see anyone coming immediately, and indicated that I was about to move into the next lane and head toward the parking lot. A truck was coming down the lane, so I stayed put and waited for the line to move forward. When it cleared, I backed into a parking spot, combat-parked. My 2014 C7 didn't come with front cameras yet, that was the next year's model, and let's just say my depth perception leaves something to be desired. I had already scraped and replaced the front lip spoiler three times at that point because of curbs, so backing in was the safer choice. Thank God for rear cameras.

Only a minute later, Alex came out smiling, like he always does, ready to tell me about his day. We headed home, and he was eager to open his newly arrived Amazon package, a Pokémon Prismatic Evolutions Trainer Box he'd been waiting for all week. And as we stepped into the house, I got a notification on my phone, a message from the school principal. It read:

Malinda,

Student safety is our top priority. I understand that it gets frustrating waiting in the parking lot at dismissal, and we work hard to make this process as smooth as possible. Revving your engine and trying to move lanes is absolutely unacceptable and puts adults and students in harm's way.

It has been taking Alex a long time to come out at dismissal, and several adults have addressed this with him. All teachers pull up the dismissal spreadsheet, and students are responsible for watching the sheet to see when their number enters. Teachers give reminders throughout this process to help students stay on task, and this also helps parents move through the line quickly.

Please follow up with Alex and let him know what his role in dismissal is.

Most importantly, please help us keep our dismissal lanes and parking lot a safe place for adults and students.

Thank you,
Ashlie

I was taken aback. I had absolutely no idea where this was coming from. I knew Ashlie a little more personally: we had been neighbors once, we were friends on social media, and every interaction I'd had with her had been kind. And I could tell from the rushed tone of the message (and the fact that she misspelled my name) that she had written it in haste. But still defensiveness and anger hit me like a familiar cloud. And if you don't think the enemy loves to twist the gifts God has given you and use them for sin, you're mistaken.

In the age of keyboard warriors, I know how to craft an email that could cut straight to the bone. And in that moment, my fingers filled with fire. I started typing out a scathing response, angry, sharp, ready for war. Then I paused.

I decided to call the school and speak to her directly instead. How dare she send me a message like that? How dare she assume anything about me? I wasn't frustrated waiting for Alex. I wasn't revving my engine out of anger. But now? Now I was mad. When Ashlie answered the phone, there was no grace in my voice. No humility. No desire for understanding. I didn't call to find peace. I called because I wanted justice. I called because I wanted to put her in her place. It was an attack posture derived from defensiveness, and it had never served me well. Deep down, I knew it came from a place of fear and rejection, not righteousness.

I told her she was way out of line and presumptuous for sending that email. I explained that I wasn't trying to change lanes out of impatience; I was following what the teacher instructed. And as for revving my engine? Seriously. I explained that I drive a modified V8 Corvette, with a manual transmission. When you're crawling in a line like that, you have to feather the gas in first gear or the car will stall. And yes, it's loud. It's supposed to be. But at no point was I "revving" in frustration or aggression. "If I had really revved my engine," I told her, "everyone inside that building would've heard it and felt it."

I also demanded an apology for the hasty and uninformed assumptions made about me. She didn't respond well at first, insisting she would not apologize for advocating for the safety of her staff and students, and that made me even more angry. I would never and have never put anyone in danger simply by driving my car.

Ashlie perceived I was doing something I wasn't doing, and perceptions can deceive. In the military, people would say "perception is reality" to justify uniformed accusations and idiotic orders. I hated it then; I hate it now.

I took Ashlie's words personally. Eventually, Ashlie and I both calmed down. I asked her, respectfully now, to next time seek understanding before firing off a message like that, not just with me but with any parent. I asked her to please explain to her staff that not all cars sound the same, that my car wasn't being driven recklessly; it was just built differently.

And the truth was, it was never really about the car. It was about me. I wasn't reckless. I wasn't dangerous. I was just built differently. All my life, I had been misunderstood, labeled as too much, too loud, too complicated. Misread as trouble when really, I was just carrying a different wiring, a different fire, a different kind of soul. Even though my history of trauma, abuse, and neglect was demanding justice, the reality was nine-year-old Melinda was still screaming underneath it all, still desperate to be seen, to be heard, to be understood. I hung up feeling like I had won. I had defended myself and had put her in her place. But almost instantly, a heavy conviction settled on my chest. I had just done to her the very thing that wounded me so often: I had perceived an attack and responded with one.

This is a daily battle. This is why I can't fight with my own strength. "All our righteous acts are like filthy rags" (Isaiah 64:6). Even my "right" actions, even when I feel justified, are still tainted if they're not surrendered. I need His Word every day. I need the full armor of God (truth, righteousness, peace, faith, salvation, and the Spirit), because my own strength had never been enough to hold me together.

When I finally released the need to be seen by the men who shaped me, I began to see myself. Not as a reflection. Not as a reaction. But as a woman becoming her own name, her own voice, her own creation in Christ. I don't know the exact moment it happened, maybe somewhere between grief and grace, or maybe in the quiet where I stopped begging for validation, but something in me shifted. I was done being an echo.

That's when I chose to rename myself, not to erase my past but to declare that it no longer owned me. Like my old middle name, Seda, the name Sehar carried the first part of my mother's name, Seval, and the first part of my biological father's name, Hardy. What once symbolized secrecy and shame became a declaration of redemption and identity. A name born from both of them but reclaimed by me.

In Arabic, Sehar comes from the root S-H-R and means "the time before dawn," the sacred stillness when the world holds its breath just before the first light breaks the horizon. It is the place between darkness and light, the threshold where transformation begins. Just as God renamed Sarai to Sarah, and Jacob to Israel, I changed my middle name to Sehar. When God gives a new name, it isn't a correction; it's a calling. It's not about forgetting who you've been but stepping fully into who you were always meant to become.

For me, Sehar is more than a name. It is a divine invitation to rise. To let go of shame. To walk in righteousness. To live as someone chosen, seen, and renamed by the mouth of the Lord. This name wasn't given by man. It didn't come from lineage or culture or convenience. It was whispered in the stillness of surrender. It came after the fire. After the breaking. After the echo. It came with the dawn.

Sehar is my symbol of renewal, the endless possibilities God has set before me. It is the sound of my own footsteps stepping into a new beginning. It means *New Beginnings*. And for the first time, I am choosing to be more than the echo of my past. I am stepping into the light of God's purpose for me.

This is the moment everything shifts, the moment you wake up and realize you are not powerless. Not against sin. Not against addiction. Not against the battles raging in your mind. You have authority. You have a Father who loves you fiercely, who fights for you, who calls you His own, and who gives you a new name.

Author's Note

S CRIPTURE TELLS US, *"THOUGH the righteous fall seven times, they rise again"* (Proverbs 24:16). For much of my life, I misunderstood that verse. I assumed righteousness meant fewer falls, cleaner choices, steadier faith, better control. But that was never the point.

The point was always rising.

This book is not the story of a woman who figured life out quickly, or who walked a straight and faithful path without stumbling. It is the story of a woman who fell, a lot, and who learned, slowly and imperfectly, how to get back up and run toward God again and again.

"The name of the Lord is a strong tower; the righteous run to it and are safe" (Proverbs 18:10). I used to believe that verse was for people who already felt strong. Now I know it is for those who are desperate, weary, and running on wounded legs. It is not the strength of the runner that saves them, but the strength of the tower they are running toward.

If there is righteousness reflected in these pages, it is not found in my decisions or discipline, but in my return. In the choosing, sometimes crawling, sometimes angry, often unsure, to turn back toward God rather than away from Him.

If you see yourself in this story, I hope you hear this clearly: your falls do not disqualify you. They never have. What matters is not how many times you've hit the ground, but whether you are still willing to rise and run toward the One who has always been standing, waiting, and strong enough to receive you.

This is not a story about getting it right.

It is a story about getting back up.

Since the completion of this manuscript, reconciliation has begun in a place I once believed was too fractured to heal. Norma and I have reconnected in a way marked by honesty, humility, and grace. She offered me a safe space to share how I truly felt. She was willing and ready to listen, to understand, and to allow herself to be seen. I, in turn, was able to listen and understand her more fully as well.

This moment does not erase the pain described in these pages, nor does it rewrite the past. Rather, it affirms the very purpose of this book: healing through truth, honesty without minimization, and restoration made possible by love.

My prayer is that this serves as encouragement to others, that even after deep hurt, misunderstanding, and long seasons of silence, the love and grace of God remain capable of restoring what seems beyond repair. Healing is not always immediate, nor is reconciliation guaranteed, but when truth is brought into the light and hearts are willing, God is faithful to redeem and restore all things.

A LL HONOR, GLORY, power, and praise belong to our Lord Jesus Christ, *who was, and is, and is to come.* Jesus, You never stopped loving me. You waited patiently for me, saw me when no one else could see any goodness, and held me when I could not hold myself together. *In You I live and move and have my being.* This story exists because You do.

To my three sons, Austin, Jacob, and Alexander, you are the reason this story matters. You are living evidence of God's love on earth and the clearest expression of purpose I have ever known. Through you, I learned what real, unconditional love looks like. I am beyond proud of each of you and the young men you are becoming. *Keep God first in all you do, and He will make your paths straight.*

To my parents, thank you for bringing me into this world and for doing the best you could with what you had. I wish there had been less stigma around mental health and more awareness, understanding, and support like what exists today. I pray you find safe spaces to process the hurt and pain I know you have endured as well.

To my dear sister, I love you very much and continually pray for healing and restoration in your life. I hope this book offers understanding, and that one day you may feel free to open your heart and share your own perspective too.

To the professors, mentors, and leaders who shaped me along the way, Dr. Robinson, Dr. Crawford, Dr. Leonard, Mr. Palmer, Mr. Foster, Mr. Hunt, Coach Rod, 1SG Whittington, CPT Smith, and General Dempsey, thank you. You are brilliant men of integrity and wisdom who made me feel safe, heard, and seen. What you poured into me, I now pass down to my sons, in the hope that they, too, will grow into men of courage, humility, and character.

To Rebecca and Nancy, who walked beside me quietly during the darkest season of my life, thank you. Your friendship came without strings or expectations. You understood my limitations, honored my capacity, and met me exactly where I was. You are gifts from Jesus, and I am eternally grateful for you both.

The Hour of Sehar

Father God,
I come before You not with perfection, but with honesty.
Not with a polished past, but with a present that aches for Your presence.
I bring You my brokenness, my wounds, my regrets, my questions, my shame
and I lay them at Your feet.

I am tired of running.
I am ready to be still in Your grace.
Ready to stop hiding and start healing.
Ready to believe that I was never too far gone for Your love to reach me.

You know every part of my story,
the pages I tore out, the chapters I skipped, the secrets I buried.
And still, You call me Yours.

So today, I surrender.
Not just my sin, but my striving.
Not just my failures, but the lies that have chained me to them.

I surrender my name, my pain, and my past.
And I ask You, Jesus, write something new.

Make me whole, not by my strength, but by Your mercy.
Refine me like gold in Your fire.
Renew me like the morning You spoke into existence.
Restore to me the joy of being fully known, fully forgiven, and fully loved.

Let this be my Sehar, my sacred hour of awakening.
Not an end, but a beginning.
Not a moment of shame, but a doorway into redemption.

I no longer want to echo what was.
I want to rise into what is
into who You say I am.

Jesus, You are my hope.
You are my healer.
You are my salvation.
You are the only name that can make dead things live again.

In Your mighty, beautiful, matchless name I pray,
Amen.

www.ingramcontent.com/pod-product-compliance
Lightning Source LLC
Chambersburg PA
CBHW031143130726
47988CB00006B/2500